The Thistle Inn

A Wee Bit of Scotland in Maine

Hilary E. Bartlett

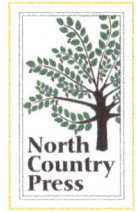

The Thistle Inn

Copyright © 2020 by Hilary E. Bartlett

All rights reserved. No part of this book may be reproduced or transmitted in any form or by any means without written permission of the author.

ISBN 978-1-943424-56-6

Library of Congress Control Number: 2019953597

Front Cover: Leonie Greenwood-Adams, proprietor of the Thistle Inn, 1963-1981. Stephen Rubicam.

Back Cover: Oak Street view of the Thistle Inn. Hilary E. Bartlett, 2018.

North Country Press
126 Main Street
P.O. Box 501
Unity, Maine 04988
www.northcountrypress.com

In memory of the late Leonie Greenwood-Adams and T'Donald Booth Morren, proprietors of the Thistle Inn (1960s and '70s) as well as staff and patrons who have passed on.

I cook with wine, sometimes I even add it to the food.
—W. C. Fields

I feel bad for people who don't drink.
When they wake up in the morning
that's as good as they're going to feel all day.
—Frank Sinatra

There comes a time in every woman's life when
the only thing that helps is a glass of champagne.
—Bette Davis

So life goes on in Boozebay Harbor.
—Leonie Greenwood-Adams

I set out to write about the Thistle Inn in the 1960s and '70s, but as I dredged up memories with friends, my book evolved into a love letter to Boothbay Harbor. Stories about the owner, Leonie Greenwood-Adams—a fascinating character who married five times—are woven with my own, why I, a city girl from England, chose to stay in a Maine coastal village and what the Thistle Inn meant to me.

Stories in this memoir may play with complete accuracy because of inconsistency of memory, but where possible I have endeavored to verify facts. Names have been omitted from some tales in order to protect people's privacy.

TABLE OF CONTENTS

ACKNOWLEDGEMENTS 1

INTRODUCTION 3

T'DONALD'S TIME (1963-1967) 9

LEONIE PICKS UP THE REINS (1968-1981) 34

LEONIE BOWS OUT (1981-1982) 109

A NEW ERA (1982-present) 116

CONCLUSION 119

BIBLIOGRAPHY 121

APPENDICES 123
   1. Regional Map 123
   2. Downtown map of Boothbay Harbor 124
   3. 1885 Map 126
   4. Obituary for T'Donald 127
   5. Top of 1966 menu cover 128
   6. 1966 menu 129
   7. 1978 menu 135
   8. Leonie's letter to *Boothbay Register*, January 8, 1976 141
   9. Obituary for Leonie Geenwood-Adams 144

ABOUT THE AUTHOR 146

ACKNOWLEDGEMENTS

I want to thank everyone who shared stories or lent me photographs: William Balch, Elizabeth Bass, Mitch Billis, George Bourette, Kay Brown, Jeffrey Brown, Bruce Burnham, Douglas and Rebecca Carter, Lee (Rusty) Court, Bruce Crosby, Edee Deen, Lee Doggett, June Elderkin, Helen Farnham, Nancy Gaecklin, Merritt Grover, William Hallinan, Patricia Irish, Phillip and Mary Lou Koskela, Peter Larsen, Connie Manter, Lucille Machon, Dana Moses, David and Suzanne Norton, Karen Perkins, David Phinney, Anya and Dick Reid, Nadeen and David Reinecke, Robert Rice, June Campbell Rose, Patricia Royall, William Royall, Stephen Rubicam, Linda and Carmen Sapienza, Jeffrey Savastano, Rhonda Selvin, Terry and Lauren Stockwell, Bruce Tindal, J. D. Warren, Strohn Woodard, Maude Wright.

I honed my writing skills thanks to a fellowship given by the Waypoint Foundation and time spent at one of their Key Largo retreats. Heartfelt appreciation is given to author Cheryl Blaydon and freelance writers Linda Sapienza and Strohn Woodard who offered their insights on early drafts of this manuscript. I am also grateful to Anya and Dick Reid, current proprietors of the Thistle Inn, who allowed me to photograph and measure for a floor plan. I also want to thank those who offered technical assistance and helped with research: Barbara Rumsey, curator of Boothbay Regional Historical Society; the staff at the *Boothbay Register*; Boothbay Region Chamber of Commerce; HarborTech Solutions; Boothbay Harbor Memorial Library; and Southport Memorial Library.

Special thanks are given to Patricia Newell, my publisher at North Country Press, for patiently guiding me through the process.

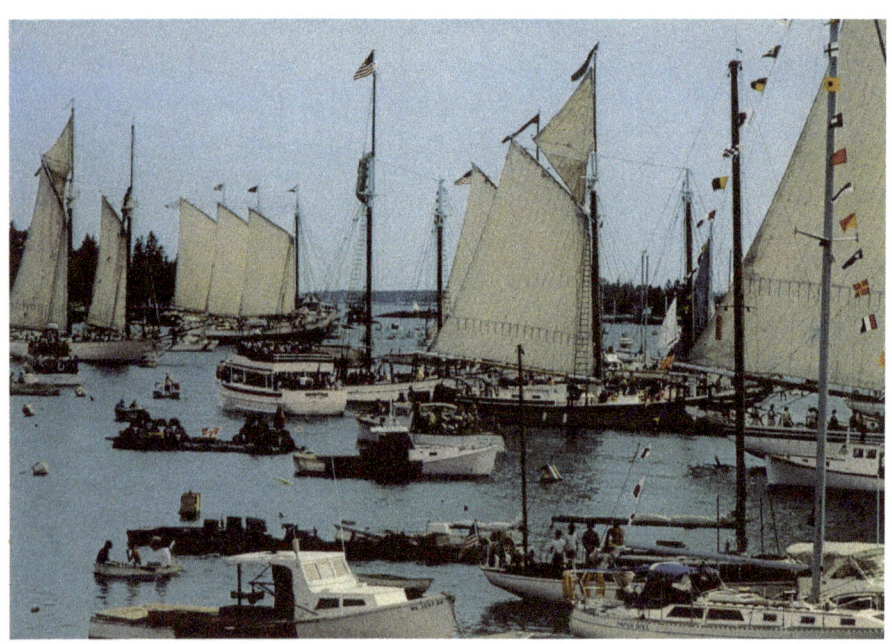

Windjammer Days, Boothbay Harbor. Ed Elvidge. Mid-1960s. (Courtesy of Boothbay Region Historical Society)

INTRODUCTION

The Thistle Inn is in Boothbay Harbor, a fishing community at the tip of a fifteen-mile rocky peninsula in Midcoast Maine — a place I fell in love with in my twenties and now call home.

The region was once called Townsend after Lord Townshend, who was nicknamed Champagne Charley because of a drunken speech in the House of Lords. Scotch-Irish immigrants reclaimed land to farm after decades of French and Indian wars. The area was incorporated into Boothbay in 1764. Settlers turned to the sea when stony soil failed to provide enough food. By the 1820s, fishing and shipbuilding were a backbone of trade. The spectacular scenery also attracted tourists.

Present day visitors crave steamed lobsters and they sail where bright buoys bob on a windswept bay. Summer folk boost our economy and locals reclaim Boothbay Harbor after fall when storm windows are put in place, logs are split and stacked. We hunker down for another 'wicked cold' winter.

The Thistle Inn pulls us on Friday nights when the town lies under a blanket of snow.

The house that became the Thistle Inn was built on Oak Street in 1861 for Captain Samuel Miller Reed. (1885 map, p 126) He was lost at sea two years later. Taxes were assumed by his heirs and the property was conveyed to Captain Gilman Low, who introduced regular steamboat service between Bath and Boothbay. He lived at the Oak Street house until he died in 1919.

Ralph Colby bought the residence in the early 1930s. His daughter, Lucille, lived there when she was in high school. I met Lucille and recognized her. She worked at the post office when I lived downtown.

"My father was a chief engineer, he went to sea. When we bought the house they always told us that a captain, kind of a queer guy, had died there and we daren't go up to the attic for a long time. I graduated eighty-four years ago; that's a lifetime, more than a lifetime. It was two-way traffic then on Oak Street and a whole box of codfish was thirty-nine cents." Lucille's mouth drooped when she talked of the Depression. "I've seen the time when the men wanted it to snow so they could earn some money shoveling."

An open field stretched from Lucille Colby's porch to Smith Street and Townsend Avenue (before they extended Union Street). Children coasted downhill on a snowy crust towards her father's two-pump filling station.

"They're all oak trees," she said and passed me a photo of the house. "And when the leaves came down my father used to rake 'em and put 'em in a pile. He'd light 'em and all the kids came over."

Lucille pointed to the far end of the residence that faced Townsend Avenue. "That's where the outhouse was."

The family kept their Dodge in a barn on Oak Street (now the Thistle Inn's dining rooms). A smelt shanty was stored in the back. The property was sold to the YMCA in the mid-fifties. They replaced the barn door with a regular one and the outbuilding was rented out.

Boothbay Harbor was more self-sufficient in the early 1960s and you could buy almost everything in town. For entertainment there was an opera house and a Strand movie theater. Inhabitants rarely left the peninsula. Old folk recalled a time before the swing bridge was built and Southport Island residents came by boat to Boothbay Harbor.

Oak Street is lined with white clapboard houses and broad-leafed trees, one of two roads in a one-way traffic system. The Thistle Inn stands on a corner with Union Street which leads to the Head of the Harbor. Oak Street bends towards the west side of the bay — a port of call where ferries dock and boats tie up at a public town landing.

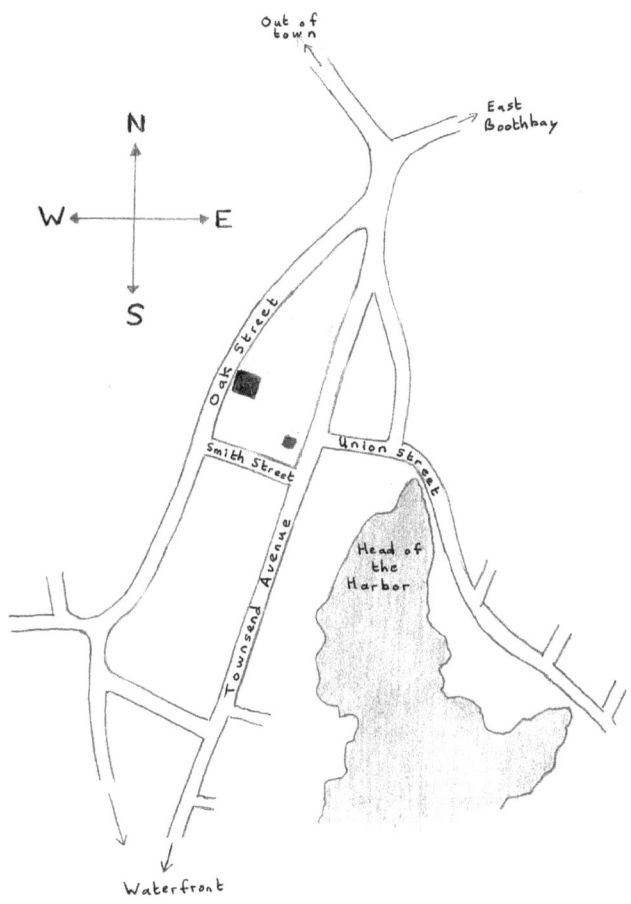

Colby's residence that became the Thistle Inn (large black square) and Colby's filling station (small black square). Hilary E. Bartlett

A Scotsman, Donald Booth Morren (T'Donald), and his wife, Leonie (Lee-OH-nee) fell in love with the sea captain's house at 55 Oak Street and bought the property in 1962. T'Donald was also smitten by the scenery, which reminded him of the east coast of Scotland. At last he had found the perfect place for an inn. He named it The Thistle Inn after his country's national flower.

Boothbay Harbor had always been a second home for Leonie — she had vacationed there since childhood. She was born of Australian parents

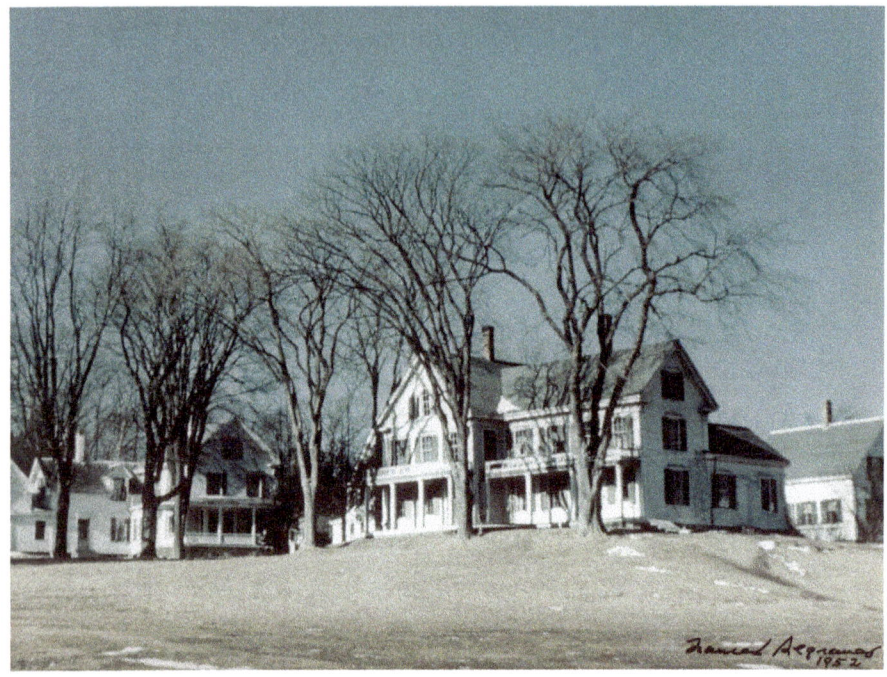

55 Oak Street (Colby's residence) before the Union Street extension was built. 1952. Daniel Argraves. (Courtesy of Dick and Anya Reid)

in 1924 in New York City. Her father, Marmion Greenwood-Adams, was an author and lecturer. Her mother, Irma, was a classically trained singer. Leonie was named after her famous grandfather, León Caron, a French composer and violinist who went to Australia and conducted at Melbourne Opera House. She attended high school in Flushing (Queens) and a business college on Long Island. Leonie blazed trails for women in the mid-1940s as a freelance travel writer, with articles in Australia's *Sydney Morning Herald,* as well as British and American magazines: *Time and Tide, Collier's Weekly,* and *Holiday.* She worked with photographer Earl Leaf and wrote stories about their adventures, such as

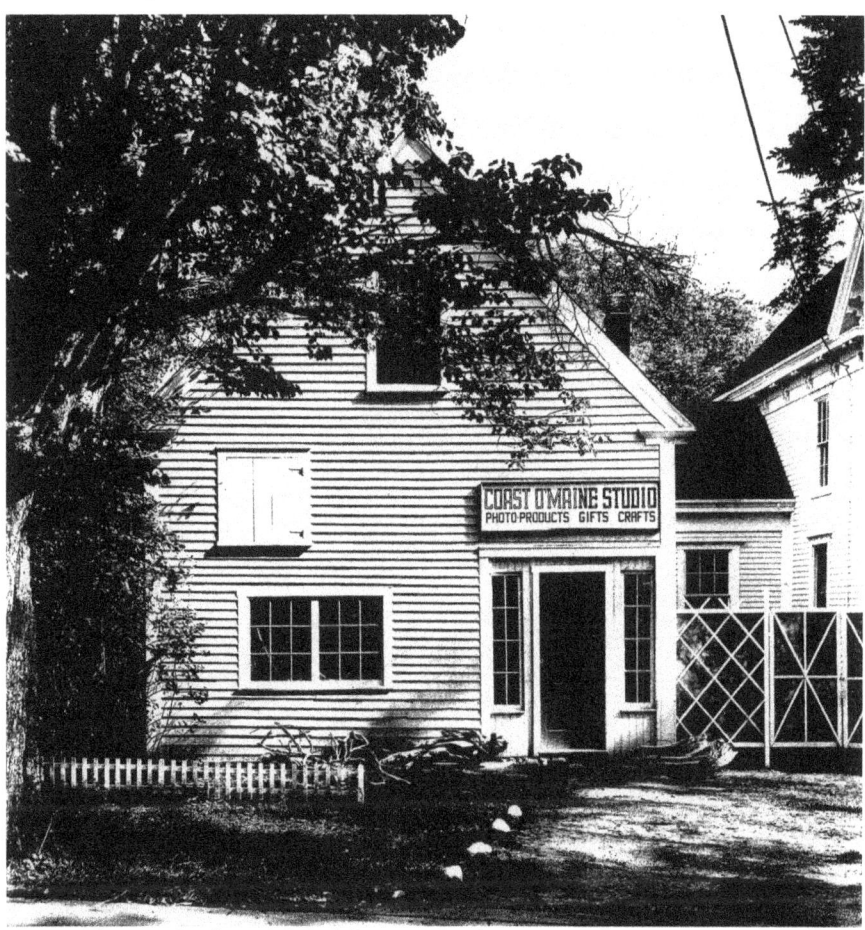

Coast O'Maine Studio at 55 Oak Street. The door is now the entrance to the Thistle Inn's front dining room. The pub was built in the fenced courtyard. 1950s. (Courtesy of Dick and Anya Reid)

a midnight Voodoo ceremony deep in the hill country of Haiti, in an era when the practice was officially banned.

Earl Leaf credited his beautiful young assistant for a successful trip to South America. "Leonie toted cameras, harangued reluctant models, maneuvered flash extensions, argued with taxi drivers, kept caption notes, did most research, and wrapped cabinet ministers, presidents, and other official ilk around her finger."

Leonie subsequently worked for Pan Am and was a continuity editor for ABC in Hollywood. She was an executive secretary on Madison Avenue and a copy writer at New York's WOR Radio. Leonie had been married twice before she wed T'Donald in Manhattan. This was his second marriage and he had a son by his first wife.

T'Donald was born in 1926 to Evelyn and William Booth Morren. His father had been in the Royal Scots during WWI. He became Chief Constable of Edinburgh City Police and was knighted by the Queen. T'Donald came to the U.S. in 1954, a year after his father was made Lord High Constable of Scotland.

Nadeen Reinecke, T'Donald's niece, said that he rarely mentioned his parents or upper-crust background. "I don't think he was overly comfortable in the stereotypical role of the Scotsman at home," Nadeen said. "I think he was happier here in the United States with a little bit more informality and his older brother would have inherited the property and title."

The Boothbay Region claimed to be New England's capital of boating. Tourism was on an upswing in the early 1960s and numbers of transient overnight guests had risen in the off-season. T'Donald and Leonie wanted to tap into that market. Since motels were all the rage, they called the Thistle a Motor Inn in their first brochure. There were larger seasonal hotels but the Thistle Inn intended to stay open in winter with a pub and a fully licensed restaurant. The inn's proprietors were from New York and townsfolk were wary of strangers. T'Donald and Leonie needed to woo locals.

T'DONALD'S TIME (1963-1967)

Leonie, T'Donald and their beagle set up home in the gable end of the house on the third floor. The Thistle Inn opened for business in July 1963. Edee Deen took care of the dog while she did morning chores. "Bonnie was cute," she recalled. A gnarled lilac bush shaded part of the newly paved parking lot on Oak Street. The front of the house faced south towards Union Street. Boarders entered through a door on the front porch. A staircase in the hallway led to rooms on the second and third floors. There were nine rooms, and room four and five connected. Guests shared bathrooms except for room one, a suite on ground level. Opposite this was a living room with a library. T'Donald was Chef when they first opened the inn. He cooked a house special each evening and a man-sized breakfast was included in the price of a room. Picnics could be ordered as well as light lunches and Scottish teas.

Daily Accommodation Rates

Singles	from $4.00 to $6.00
Doubles	from $8.00 to $11.50
Family Rooms	$16.50 for family of four
Bed and full board	(3 meals per day) rates advised on request

10% discount for 7 or more consecutive days. Economical out of season rates.

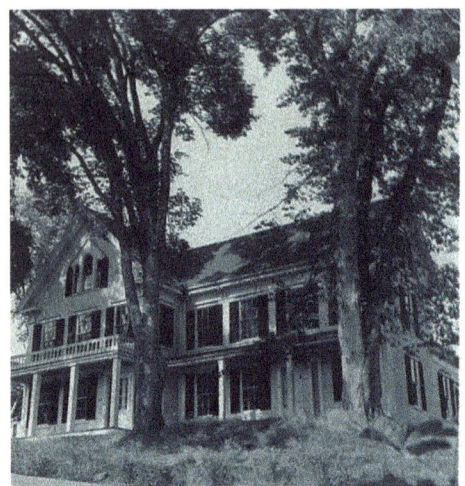

The Thistle Inn

The Thistle Inn
A Home Away From Home

In the heart of
Boothbay Harbor, Maine
Telephone 1051

Thistle Inn's 1963 brochure cover. (Courtesy of Dick and Anya Reid)

T'Donald hired laborers to add dormers to the south roof for four guest rooms on the top level. Clapboards were painted a light shade of lavender set off by dark shutters. Leonie and T'Donald reconfigured space in the

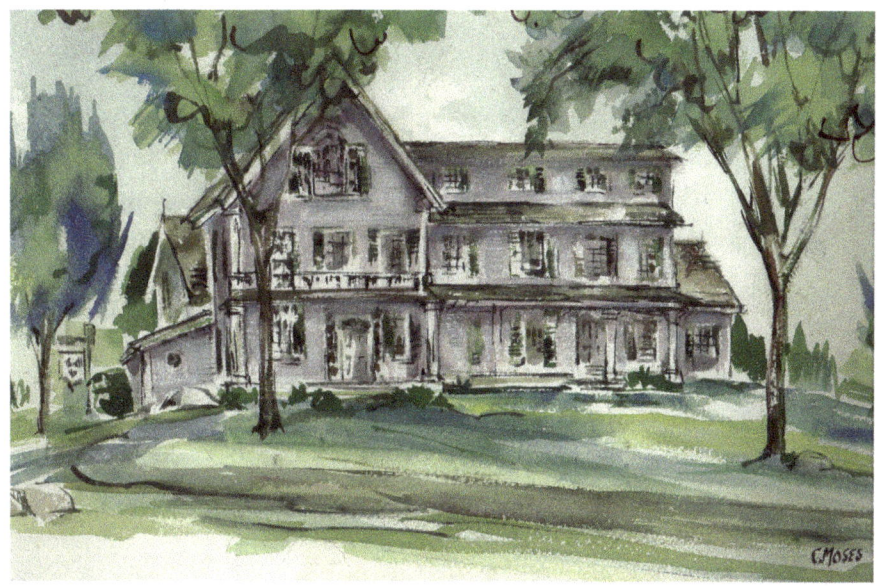

Watercolor of the Thistle Inn by Connie Moses. Mid-1960s. (Courtesy of Dick and Anya Reid)

barn to make two dining rooms and a crew built a pub between the house and barn. Dark wooden beams spanned a low hung ceiling in the front dining room and a wood stove was installed for winter. Wooden booths ran along two walls and a few square tables were in the center. English prints decorated the walls — gentlemen in powdered wigs who drank from tankards or smoked clay pipes, a few hounds resting at their feet. A doorway at the far end led to a second eating area. The Harness Room had a high peaked ceiling, benches lined two walls, and tables could be pushed together to accommodate larger groups. Leonie hung a horse harness on one wall and an oil painting of a racing driver with a trotter on the other. Both dining rooms had red plaid curtains and cushions. In those early days the kitchen was up two steps off the Harness Room. In April, 1964, the Thistle Inn's restaurant was ready for business.

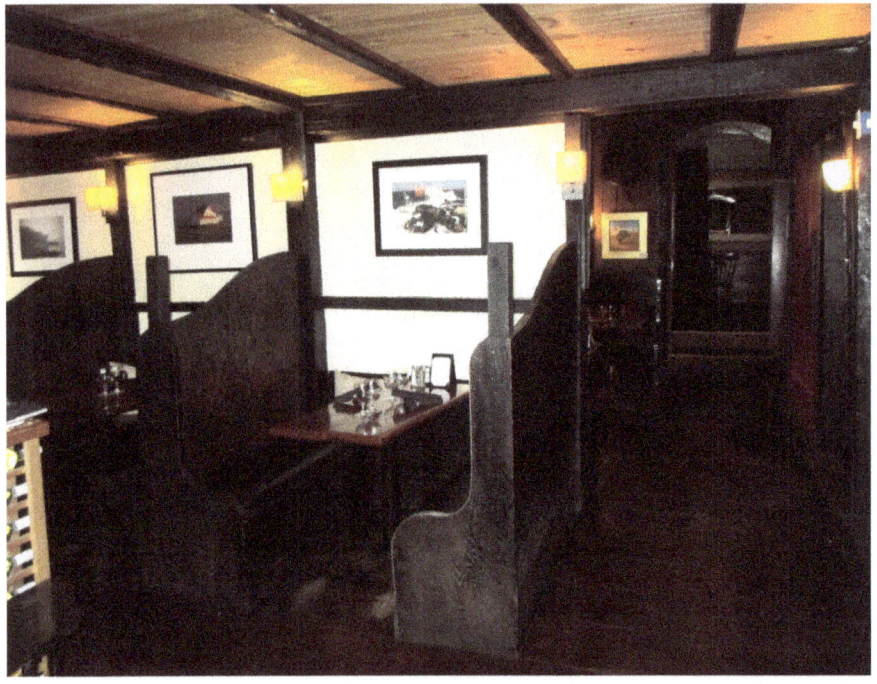

The Thistle's front dining room from Oak Street entrance. 2018. Hilary E. Bartlett.

The *Region Aire* ran an article about the Thistle. "Many are familiar with store hours and businesses that remain open throughout the winter; however, some still may not be aware that we have several new businesses remaining open this year. One such is the Thistle Inn and Restaurant. The Inn which offers rooms by the day or week also makes known that they have fine facilities for special parties."

"Everyone in town thought they were crazy to buy a drafty old house and open a restaurant," June Elderkin, a fisherman's wife, said. "We went over right off when they started servin' food and we were told we could bring our own booze. They'd bring us a set-up—ice in a glass and water, whatever—and the food was absolutely out of this world. We couldn't wait until they got a liquor license 'cause we liked to go out back in those days. We didn't have a gang of kids then and we went out a lot, but the food was wonderful and of course T'Donald and Leonie were very colorful."

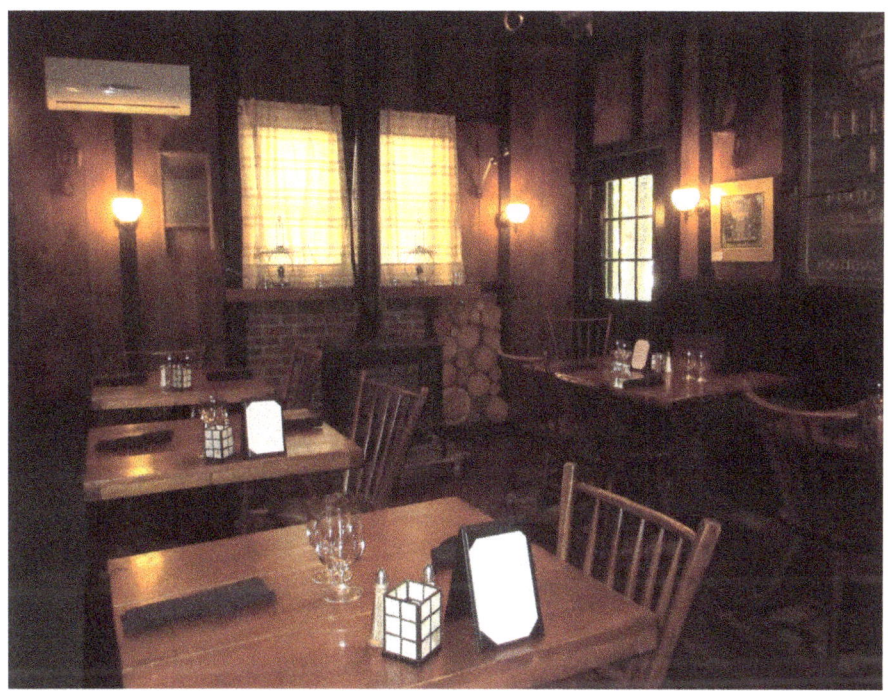

Harness Room at the Thistle. 2018. Hilary E. Bartlett.

The outside wall of the newly built pub and vestibule extended from the house by five feet, possibly to comply with an ordinance for a saloon to be far from a church (a Methodist one was close by). The Thistle was granted a liquor license. There were eateries on both sides of the harbor, but the Thistle Inn was the only licensed restaurant open in winter. Before they opened, June Elderkin and her husband had to drive fifteen miles to the Ledges Inn in Wiscasset for an evening meal and a cocktail.

Leonie's niece, Nadeen, came out from Colorado to work as a chambermaid in the summer of 1964. Nadeen met her future husband, Dave Reinecke, at the Thistle Inn. Dave, a local lad, washed dishes and made salads for T'Donald.

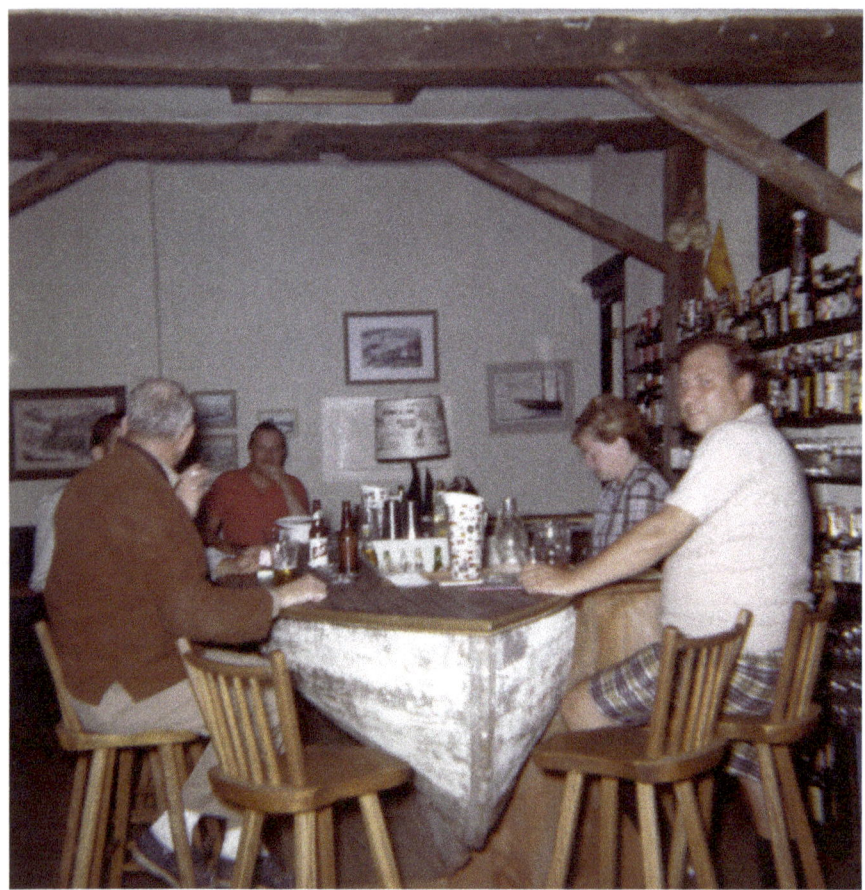

Leonie (behind the Dory Bar) and T'Donald (on her right) when the pub first opened. 1964. Nadeen Reinecke.

'Le Pub' opened that summer. T'Donald had found a wooden dory at the back of the barn and made that boat the centerpiece of his pub. He faced the bow toward a front window and added a varnished wooden top for a counter. The Dory Bar made the pub unique. Mugs hung from brace-beams above shelves of liquor and a bulbous glass tube held a yard of ale. Health regulations about stemware were less rigorous in the sixties. Glasses were washed in warm soapy water with bottle brushes, then dipped in a sink of rinse water. Servers carried trays of drinks to diners through an open barn door. At night, mellow sconce lighting softened plastered walls in the pub and reflections winked in a bay window. A chorus of voices greeted newcomers when they opened the pub door. Wisps of cigarette smoke rose up to smudge the new ceiling. On wet stormy nights, a faint smell of beer mingled with a musty odor of damp woolen clothing.

Steps at the stern of the Dory Bar led to a corridor (in the main house) with restrooms. T'Donald hung a large painting of lobster buoys by Connie Moses in the men's room. The Scotsman pronounced buoy as boy. The gents was called the b(u)oys room after that.

"May a pox be on the head of those so-called humans who stole our 'Pets Welcome' sign," Leonie said in the *Boothbay Register*. "It is neither funny nor in good taste and it shows that animals are sometimes more intelligent than people."

Bonnie, the beagle, gave birth to three lads (Angus, Jock and MacTavish) and a lassie (Heather). T'Donald was midwife. They kept only one puppy, Angus. The others were put up for adoption. Leonie referred to Angus and Bonnie as Prince and Princess Morren. Both were overweight from tidbits between meals and Leonie begged customers to refrain or offer only dog biscuits. Some ads in the *Boothbay Register* were signed with a paw print by Bonnie Beagle Greenwood-Adams or written from a dog's point of view. Others, in the *Region Aire,* featured a sketch of both beagles seated on stools at the bow of the dory.

T'Donald and Leonie launched their new sailboat in July 1964, they tacked around the harbor on Sundays and brought their beagles along for the ride. T'Donald bought his wife a white swimsuit with a flapper fringe to wear when they went for a sail. On Windjammer Day, Leonie strutted down the street to their boat in her snazzy bathing suit like Miss America.

"Aye 'tis true . . . 'twas ooour wee boatee capsized off Cabbage Island this week," Leonie said in the newspaper. "T'Donald would like to thank Ruth Levitt and her crew, plus all the others for helping him out. Bonnie and Leonie had the sense to stay onshore but Angus really knows how to swim now."

A parakeet, Prince, joined T'Donald's and Leonie's family at the inn. The bird died a few months later and was replaced by another, Prince II.

T'Donald and Leonie courted locals in an advert written in a Scottish brogue. "Do try us and also remember 85% of ooour guid customers do NOT have a drink with their lunch . . . except for a glass of cold water!" Special of the day was only $1.50, the most expensive meal was $2.65 and the least was 70 cents.

The Thistle Inn's owners worked as a team. Their enthusiasm was infectious. They ran the business, filled in behind the bar and in the kitchen, scoped out their competition, and browsed for antiques at yard sales. At one, they picked up a beady-eyed parrot on a perch and an antique sign with rules of the tavern — Bobby Rice, head bartender, recalled the time that T'Donald and Leonie carried an unwieldy sailfish down Oak Street. Nearly everything that decorated the walls of the Thistle Inn had a personal connection to the owners. Photographs of their beagles hung in the pub along with a large map of Scotland. Specialty drinks were listed on a wooden sign. Leonie's tipple was a Rusty Nail (Scotch with Drambuie) whereas her husband liked his Scotch straight or with milk.

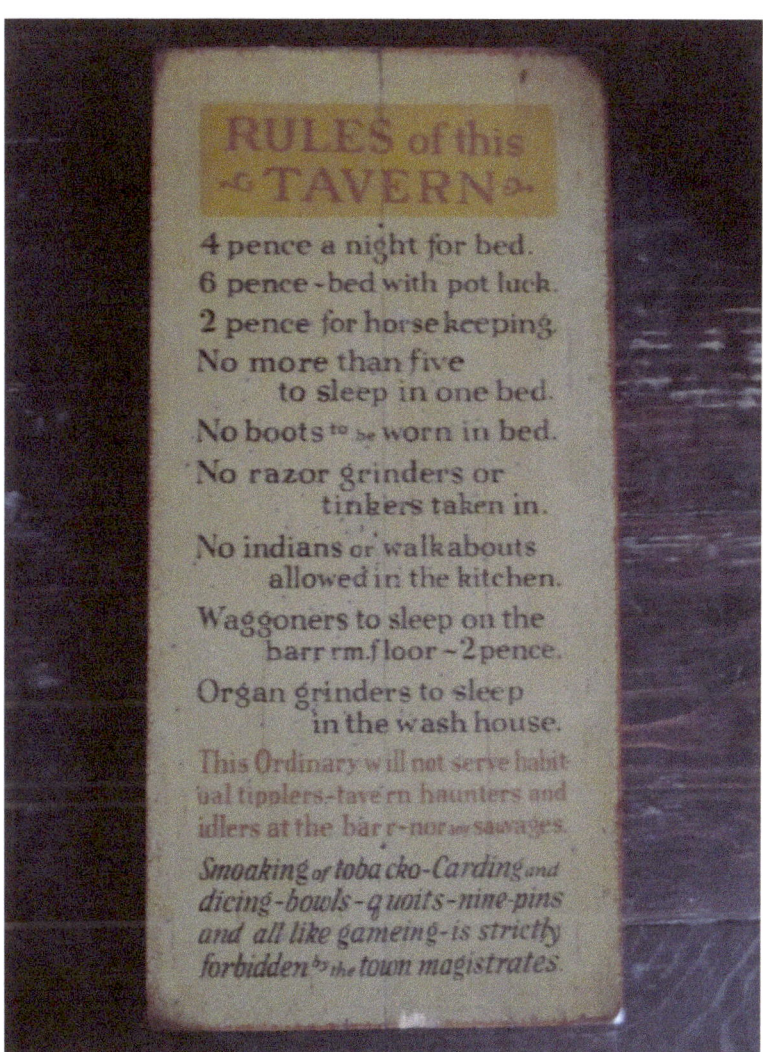

Rules of the Tavern. 2018. Hilary E. Bartlett.

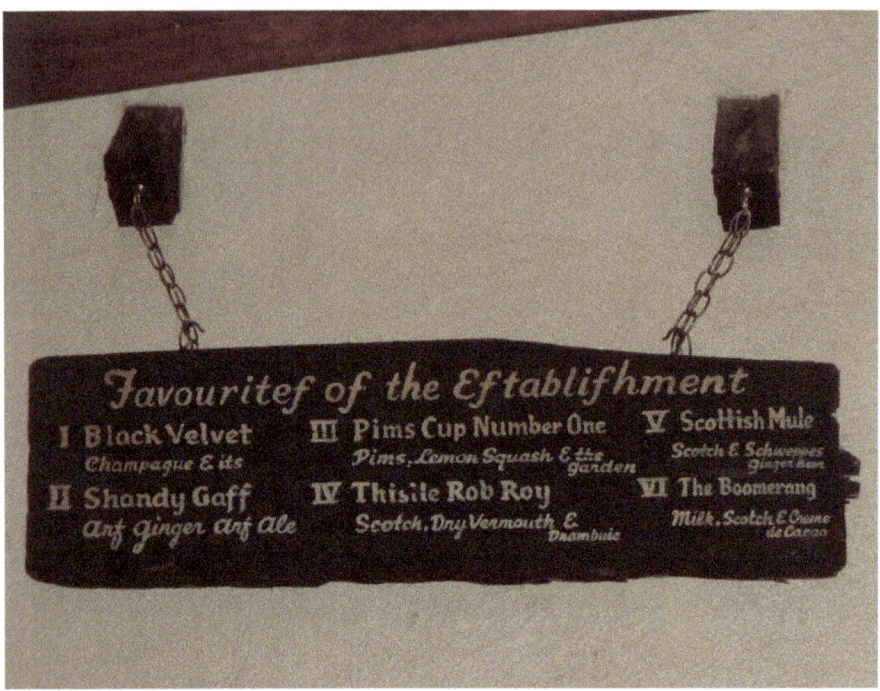

Favorites of the Establishment. 2018. Hilary E. Bartlett.

A dartboard was on a wall close to the Dory Bar. In order to get to the bar, people had to walk in front of players throwing those lethal weapons. They had to watch out at all times. When dart tournaments were held, players wore Thistle Inn T-shirts with a red and navy bullseye on the back. Sore losers claimed they had been put off their game when someone walked through to buy a drink. One dart enthusiast who owned a barge rounded up a crowd in the pub on Saturday night and took them out to Damariscove Island to play volleyball on Sunday.

Leonie's husband was a stocky broad-shouldered fellow. He greeted guests with a generous smile and introduced himself in a thick Scottish burr. His cool-headed demeanor balanced Leonie's more vivacious personality. She wore flamboyant outfits with magenta lips and nails to meet her public, dressed to the nines for the rubber boots and dungaree crowd. She might be in Boothbay Harbor but she was the girl from Manhattan whose only nod to approaching middle age was reading glasses. She cleaned them with a drop of vodka and swore that worked better than anything else.

"When Leonie came in the room you knew she was on a mission," a former employee said. "She was just goin' for it all the time."

The Thistle Inn offered amenities of a Highland country pub, where patrons could have their mail delivered. Tourists frequented the Thistle in summer; during winter months the pub was full of locals. T'Donald disregarded American bar hours and reverted to British opening times in the offseason — 5:30 to 10:30 p.m. on weeknights and up to 11:30 p.m. on Saturdays. People flocked to the Thistle after work, crammed like sardines in a can. You had to step over those who sat on stairs to reach the restrooms. Weekends were the same. Whether at lunch, Happy Hour, or dinner, the Thistle Inn was always busy. Bartenders knew everyone's usual and a blended whiskey, a martini or Manhattan could all be had for less than a dollar. Bottles of beer were fifty cents.

"If you weren't there you'd either given up drinking or you were sick," Strohn Woodard, a local, said. "They'd call you if you hadn't been in there for a while to find out if you were okay."

To further court locals, T'Donald provided various entertainment. He hired a young woman, Yo, to sing folk songs. Taped music was installed in both dining rooms. A buffet dinner dance was held on Wednesdays and Saturdays in winter for $2.25 per head. Some weekends they had a ballad singer. Other times they had a disc jockey and customers would bring their own records. An upright player piano—left by the Colby family when they sold the house—was moved into the pub. The wooden frame was soon plastered with advertisements for booze. Music rolls were stacked on top and activated by pumping pedals. At sing-a-longs on Monday nights, Leonie swore that she could play those ragtime tunes better than anyone else. She plopped down at the piano bench, fluffed up her sleeves, turned to grin at her audience and enthusiastically pumped with her feet.

"There was some truth to what she said," Strohn Woodard recalled. "Because she did it with such spirit and determination that it sounded better. Not just faster but more impulsive and more powerful. She really made those piano rolls do something they'd never done before."

Laughter and piano music bounced off wooden beams and stucco walls as customers sang old favorites and tossed back drinks. "We were living the life," said a fisherman.

June Campbell Rose, an artist and writer, reminisced about T'Donald. "He had an accent and wore a kilt," she said. "He also revealed that he had no underwear on." June threw back her head and laughed. (Undergarments were not worn with kilts in the Royal Scots, his father's regiment.) T'Donald wore his green plaid one with wool knee socks and a shirt and tie, sometimes topped with a bone button jacket. "He was just a wonderful person to talk to and filled the bill for a Scottish gentleman," June said, "an intellectual and entertaining in his own way. So I remember him with affection. He was part of the scenery and he seemed to make the place a painting. I thought, wow, it's like being in a pub in Scotland."

T'Donald mostly ran around in shorts and long black socks in summer. One of his first bartenders had incendiary red hair and was mad about Scottish culture. He wore a kilt when he worked behind the bar.

Leonie and T'Donald had a cocktail party for the Queen's official birthday on the second Saturday in June. A select few were invited to this afternoon event, held in the living room on the Thistle Inn's first floor. Women dressed in hats and gloves accompanied by men in suits, except T'Donald who proudly wore his kilt. A fisherman's wife recalled the fancy affair, "My husband dressed in his suit – *imagine*." Champagne was served along with dishes of strawberries and clotted cream. T'Donald made a toast to the Queen and fired a miniature cannon on the front lawn as a salute.

T'Donald was head chef as well as innkeeper. Four or five dishes were offered plus a daily special. He always had boiled Brussels sprouts as a fresh vegetable entrée, sometimes British mushy peas, which could be spread with a knife. He added green food dye to pep up the color if the reconstituted peas looked too bland. Roast beef was served on Wednesday nights in fall and winter. The proprietor strode into his pub in a spotless white chef's cap that erupted from his brow like an atomic mushroom cloud.

Scottish, right down to his sporran, T'Donald rolled his '*rs*'. "Verra, verra rare," he said as he pointed to a platter in his hand. Then he carved off a piece of meat and handed it to you. "An' 'tis here for dinner."

He also served a 'his and hers' strip steak and a twenty-two ounce millionaire's sirloin for connoisseurs. If a customer complained their beef was overcooked, T'Donald added a few drops of red food coloring in the kitchen then sent the dish back out. He fired himself and hired a chef. The owner, however, was back in the kitchen by winter.

"Leonie cooked too," June Elderkin said. "She was always out there putterin' around doin' stuff. But between 'em they pulled it off you know."

Several people prepared food in the Thistle's early years. Billy Royall, a teenager, was pot washer. "Even if they had an official closing time," Billy said, "by the time you started next morning the whole kitchen was full of dirty dishes again. Who knows when they really closed? You'd never seen so many and I was the only one there in the morning."

> ### THE THISTLE INN
>
> Do you know Helen Farnham at Brown Brothers or Nick at Fisherman's Wharf... well we do and they certainly give you good service. Of course, wuur rather prejudiced, but if you haven't met oour own Irene, Millie, Diane, Jan, Jane and Paul, yuuur missing a real treat, and incidentally verra guid food. We serve Breakfast, Luncheon and Dinner every day except Sunday... and we respectfully suggest ye make a reservation if ye wish ta come to dinner... 633-3541... We also serve cocktails.
>
> T'Donald and Leonie Morren

Waitresses at the Thistle Inn made $15 for two shifts, six days a week. The dining room and pub closed on Sundays. Leonie and T'Donald met Dana Moses on Monhegan Island and offered her a serving job at the Thistle. On her first night the restaurant was full. She knew all the locals and chatted with them before she took their order. T'Donald noticed service was slow and beckoned Dana at the end of her shift. "Let me buy you a drink lass, 'cause I've got to tell you yer fired."

Irene Peters, another waitress, turned out snappy tunes on the piano. Leonie gave her a write-up in the *Boothbay Register* when she left the inn. "Irene, who has been with us since we opened, we thought ye'd like ta know that she is startin' her own wee coffee shop right on the wharf this summer... So be sure to stop in to see her." Irene's café was popular for breakfast and local fishermen congregated there.

The Thistle Inn's restaurant was also busy. Some evenings they had to turn customers away. They built a new kitchen with a storeroom underneath that had a walk-in cooler. The original kitchen was converted into a Mary Queen of Scots Room to help with overflow. They closed the restaurant on June 21st and 22nd, 1965 to make the move. A service bar was set up in the new banquet room to reduce wait time for beverages ordered with a meal. Leonie asked her husband to abstain from drinking alcohol in the kitchen. T'Donald hung a liquor bottle on a piece of string outside the window and took nips while he cooked.

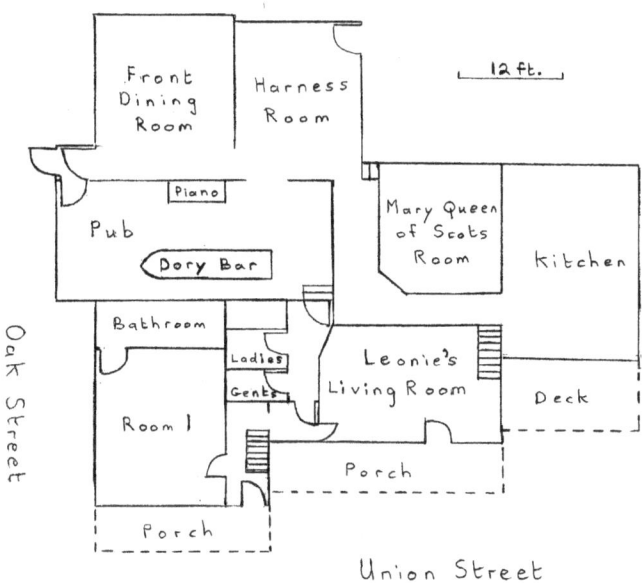

Ground floor plan of the Thistle Inn, 1966-1981. Dimensions of the Mary Queen of Scots Room, kitchen, Leonie's living room and location of back staircase were estimated due to renovations after 1981. 2018. Hilary E. Bartlett.

The Thistle's reputation grew. One night two of the cast from *The Man from U.N.C.L.E.,* (a spy-fiction TV series) came in for dinner. Leonie put this notice in the *Boothbay Register* in September, 1965. "Seen in the Harness Room a good-looking strawberry blonde, member of T.H.R.U.S.H. and handsome, suntanned man, member of

U.N.C.L.E. Are they collaborating to learn secrets of some of the Thistle's famous recipes?"

Traditional dishes were prepared on holidays, at Thanksgiving a traditional family style turkey meal. T'Donald advertised, "Dinna forget ouuur scrumptious Dinner – 'tis less work and less expensive ta eat wi' us and nay dirrrty dishes ta wash up."

Jump to 2018.

I was in the front dining room of the Thistle when Rusty Court strode over with a beaming smile under a mop of hair and bright red suspenders to match. "Hear you're writing a book about this place," he said and handed me a business card. "Give me a call." We arranged to meet at his house a few days later. A row of shirts hung from a railing by the stairs, but otherwise, his living space was that of a carefree bachelor. He cleared a place for me on a winged armchair and went down memory lane.

"I met all my wives there. I mean there wasn't many places you could have a cold beer in town then. The only other place was the Rendezvous over on Southport, which is long gone. Fifty-two years ago I was in the Coast Guard along with Leon Minzie and Larry Knowlton. And if you go in the Thistle and look above the bar, there's an oar up there that we, as Coast Guardsmen, gave Leonie back in 1965 and we all signed it. I'm surprised it's still there."

Fishermen were the largest group at the Thistle. Boothbay had been a prominent fishing center since the mid-eighteen hundreds, when factories were built to extract fish oil and can clams, sardines, mackerels, and lobster meat.

T'Donald cooked fresh fish of the day, fish and chips, plus scallop, shrimp, crab and lobster entrées. Leonie claimed that the Thistle Inn was the first pub and restaurant in Maine to treat fishermen as the first-class citizens they were. These Maine icons are tough as granite, pioneers of a last treacherous frontier. The American Bureau of Labor Statistics reported that commercial fishing is the deadliest occupation. No wonder fishermen are superstitious. They clomped into the Thistle's pub in rubber boots or waders caked in brine. Their eyes squinted from a long day's glare, faces weathered and all had tans that ended at their collars. They relaxed and played cribbage at the prow of the dory, except one old salt who preferred a barstool by the cash register at the stern. The Thistle Inn was busy when there was a 'nauth'easter or high seas and they were unable to go out. Thistle's lore was fishermen's lore – they needed each other.

A local gal talked about the vibe of the Thistle back then. "That was the place where all the fishermen went. They congregated in that corner by the dartboard and you'd hear stories and they had a very thick Maine accent. You had local color and culture there."

Four draggers fished whiting for Boothbay Harbor Freezer in the mid-sixties. Their crews drank at the Thistle. An average catch of whiting was 100,000 pounds per day during the peak. Boothbay Harbor's cold storage unit employed sixty-five to seventy people. One of those draggers was the *Lucille B*, skippered by Bob McLellan. He was interviewed for *National Fisherman* magazine in 1968. "Fishing is long hours," Bob said. "But like anything else, if you like what you're doing it's alright. Some say a fisherman is his own boss, but he really isn't . . . he's the slave of supply and demand."

George Bourette had a photograph of the *Lucille B*. I caught up with George at his home to borrow the image for my book. I parked on the side of the road, his driveway was full of vehicles. He had converted his

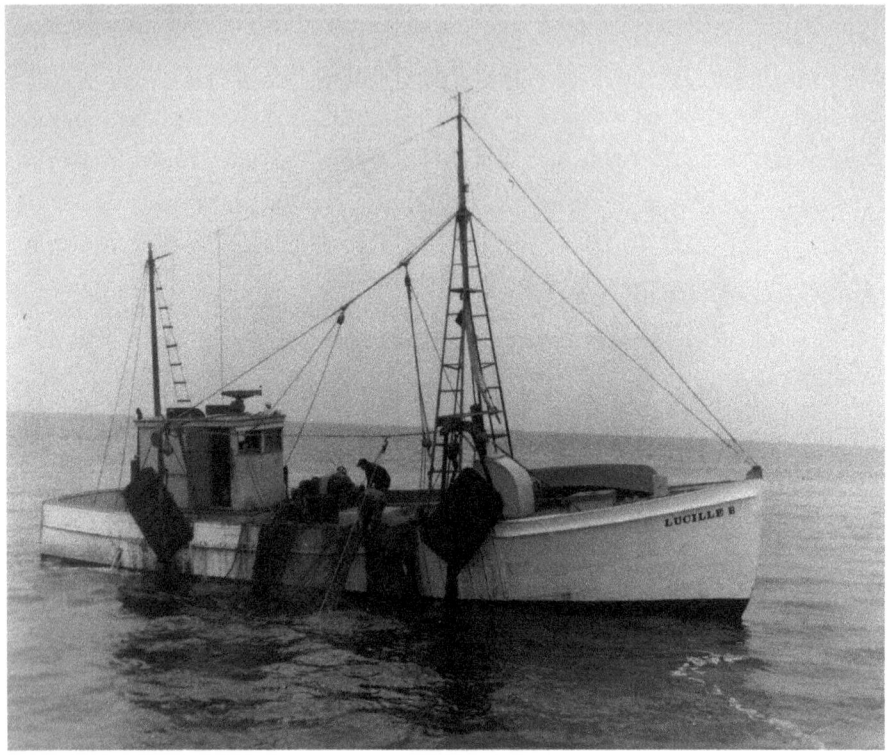

Fishing from the Lucille B. *1960s.* (Courtesy of George Bourette)

garage into a den. Doors were open and sunshine streamed in. George leaned back in a swivel chair. "Come into my office," he said with an expansive smile.

I gawked at his vast collection of memorabilia. Every inch of wall space was covered with photographs of shipyards, fishing vessels and street scenes from long ago. Like the Dory Bar at the Thistle Inn, George had a varnished boat bar in front of a cocktail set-up.

"No wonder I never see you in town," I said. "You've got everything here and you can invite your pals over."

George shrugged and smiled. He talked about the local shrimp fleet and took his photograph of the *Lucille B* off a wall.

Maine shrimp season is in winter and stocks fluctuate. They plummeted in the 1950s and boomed in the '60s. Some fishermen took advantage of high landings and put cookers onboard to steam their catch at sea. Malpeque Shrimps Ltd., a Canadian company, opened a processing plant at Jimmy Juliano's dock on the east side of Boothbay Harbor (subsequently called the Sea Pier). Malpeque bought 8,000 - 10,000 pounds of shrimp from every boat that fished for them. Portland trawlers also unloaded their catch at Boothbay Harbor's packing plant. Their crews stayed at the Thistle.

Rusty Court also filled me in on shrimping then. "When those guys were fishing you couldn't hardly buy a drink in the Thistle. They'd throw some hundred dollar bills on the bar and say, 'Hey let's have some drinks for everybody.' "

June Elderkin, now a Southport Island artist, lived in Boothbay Harbor in the mid-sixties and worked at the Thistle. "I tended bar for a while, the place was packed every night. You could barely move. That's when Malpeque was in town and the guys brought in a mess of shrimp and put 'em on the bar for a treat. They shipped 'em all over the place and you know what they did? They cooked 'em in the shells with red dye. The shrimp were more red than pink. I didn't work at the Thistle very long but I was there long enough to know that I didn't want to do that forever 'cause it was killin' me and I had a family. I fished with my husband."

Malpeque had a huge European market which only wanted shrimp that fit over the rim of a cocktail glass. The rest were discarded.

"There was the small stuff too," Terry Stockwell said. He worked for Brewer's boatyard, fished for twenty years and is now on New England's Fishery Management Council. "They didn't have great specifications then and the mesh size was smaller so everything came in." Most of the rejected shellfish ended up at the town dump. Rotting piles were pecked by gulls.

"The reality is commercial fishing is what made the Thistle Inn operate year-round financially," said Dick Reid, current proprietor of the

Thistle Inn. "My godfather ran a deep-sea drag boat out of Boothbay Harbor. I remember him saying to me, 'When the boys came into port, they'd get off and go directly to the Thistle. They rented rooms and stayed for the weekend. They got back on the boat Monday morning but they didn't have a penny left in their pockets because they'd spent it at the Thistle.' "

"It was the wild place where the wild things went," Dick's wife, Anya, said.

"Remember the horse tied up outside one time?" Terry Stockwell said. "There was no hitching post out there so they tied it onto a vehicle right outside the front door. It was kinda like the approach to everything about the Thistle - anything goes."

Consumers' taste in seafood has changed since the 1960s. Boothbay Harbor held a twelve-day tuna tournament for the biggest landed fish, but people rarely ate the meat. June Elderkin, a fisherman's wife, said, "You couldn't give tuna away - you couldn't get rid of it. We dumped them off Tumbler Island in the middle of Boothbay Harbor."

Lauren Stockwell added, "The very first time I came out to visit Terry he was working in a boatyard right downtown and it was in the middle of a tuna tournament. I'd never seen a fish that big. They were what - 900/1,000 pound fish hanging by their tail?"

Nearly all fish shops and restaurants in Boothbay Harbor serve tuna nowadays and sushi-grade fetches a fortune. Imagine, local fishermen used to throw them away and a bluefin North Atlantic tuna fetched $323,000 at a Japanese auction in 2018.

Maine lobsters were poverty food in colonial times and the commercial fishery only gained importance in the mid-1800s, due to a sudden success in canneries. Several lobsters were required to produce a pound of meat.

The Thistle Inn served them steamed, baked stuffed, in salad and on a roll. Scottish lobster pie was T'Donald's specialty. Lobstermen frequented the Thistle. They are fiercely territorial. A gaudy color scheme marked each man's buoys and they hunted down interlopers like sharks after blood. A fight broke out at the Dory Bar over trap lines being cut and two burly fellows rolled across a table. Chairs scraped along the floor as other guys rushed forward, real Wild West movie stuff. Leonie made one of those troublemakers the bouncer. She was like the saloonkeeper, Miss Kitty, in the TV series, *Gunsmoke.*

Rusty Court left the Coast Guard, went to Monhegan and became a fisherman. Islanders sailed seventeen miles to drink at the Thistle, their only hotel was dry. They were only occasional visitors. "I never witnessed a brawl in the Thistle," Rusty said, "we were lovers not fighters."

Whenever he and Craig Sproul came in from the island to buy provisions, they stopped at the Thistle for a cocktail. "I think at that time rum was the flavor, rum and coke," Rusty said. Two gals joined them at the Dory Bar. Their family had a cattle farm up-country and they offered the lads a reasonable price. "Whoa, sure, we'd love to buy some meat from you," said Rusty and ordered a quarter of a steer, butchered and packed. Two weeks later they met the gals in the Thistle and picked up three cartons of beef. The fishermen's mouths watered as they headed back to Monhegan to barbeque steaks for a bang-up dinner. What a let-down. They needed a chainsaw to cut into them. "Ha-Ha!" Rusty said. "We kidded about that. We certainly got hosed down on that one."

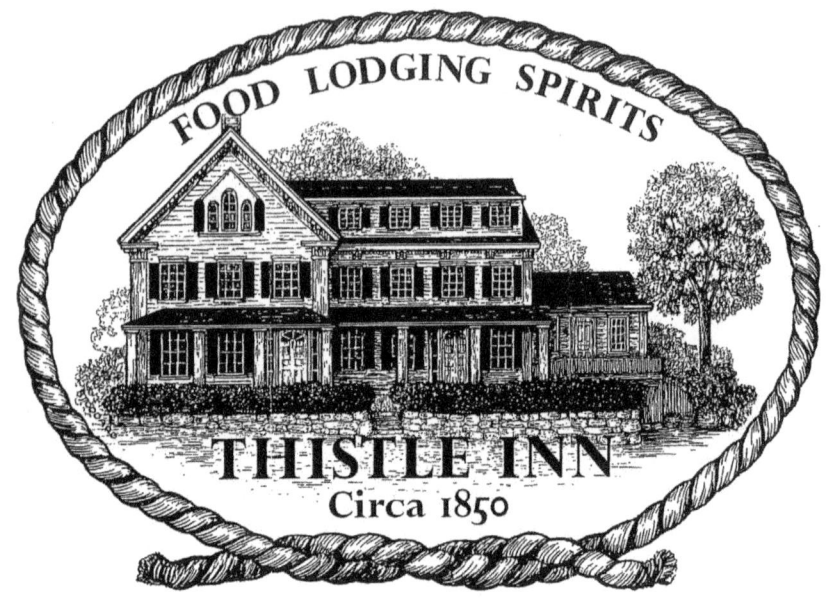

Thistle Inn's logo. 1960s. (Courtesy of Dick and Anya Reid)

Leonie commissioned a logo to be designed. She wrote letters to the editor of the *Boothbay Register*, submitted weekly notices to the classifieds and worked on the Thistle Inn's first bill of fare. Connie Moses' watercolor of the inn was used for the top of the menu cover and a drawing of a thistle was underneath. Leonie's brother and his wife had a lithography business in Colorado. They worked with Leonie to develop colors and printed her first run.

"Our new menu is so fascinating that it has already become a collector's item," Leonie claimed. Highland dishes were included: ice-cold tattie creamed soup, Kingdom of Fife pie, Scottish lobster pie, Robbie Burn's steaks and Scottish sherry trifle. Odd passages and silly sayings were scattered throughout. These had been handed down by families or T'Donald and Leonie made them up:

'WARFARE is the worst kind of fare for man to live on.'
'MODEL HUSBAND – small imitation of the real thing.'

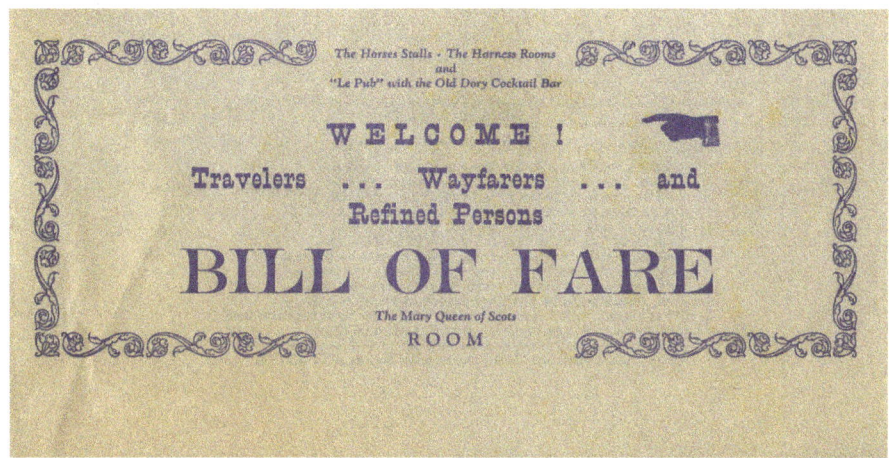

Bottom section of Thistle's 1966 menu cover. (Courtesy of Boothbay Region Historical Society)

The Thistle's cuisine attracted a well-heeled dinner crowd and despite all the upheaval in the bar, their dining rooms were always full. T'Donald and Leonie prepared food together in January 1967.

Their Scottish ad read: "Mother is nooow in the kitchen with Father so 'tis really goin' to be a surprisin' winter as far as cuisine is concerned. Just proves that when a woman loves a man trrrue blue she'll do anythin' fer him (I broke my 3-year vow not to cook!)"

Specials were still only $1.50. Gourmet meals or international cuisine were served on Wednesdays; on British Wednesdays, steak and kidney puddin', in deer season a hearty 'hunters' breakfast' starting at 4:30 a.m. They catered private parties as well, including Wiscasset Merchants Bowling League's annual dinner and Hodgdon Brothers' boat launches.

In May, 1967, the Thistle Inn put on a series of banquets for dignitaries, film crews and journalists. All had come for the launch of replica yacht, *America,* built at Goudy and Stevens' shipyard in East Boothbay.

The event made national news. Horns blared, hundreds cheered and flags fluttered as the sleek black hull slid down wooden ways into the Damariscotta River. A Shaefer brewer baron from New York had sponsored the boat and wharves were awash in Schaefer's ale.

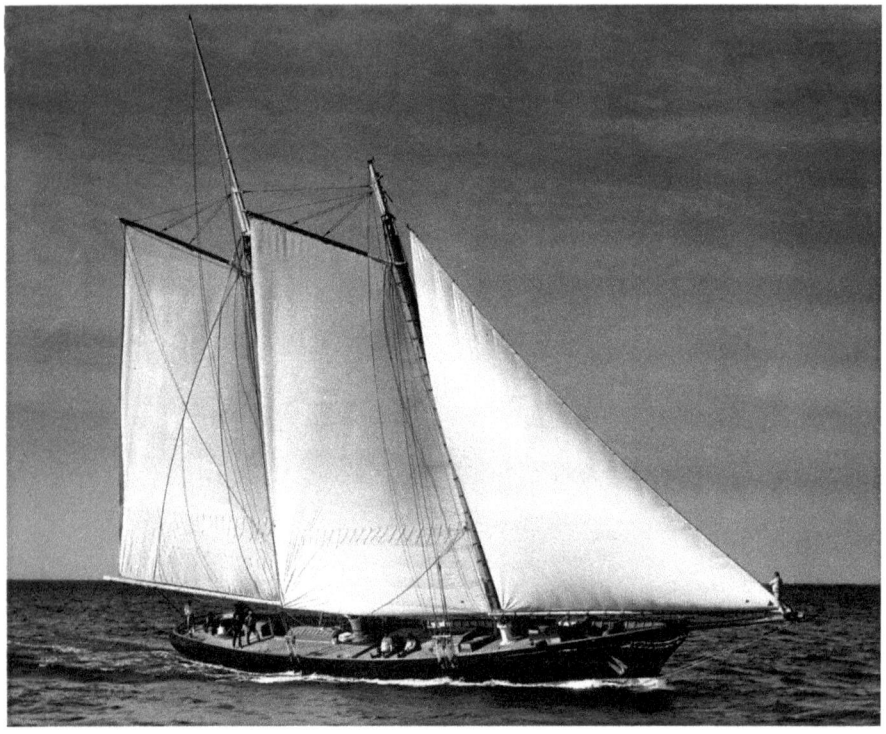

Replica yacht, America, *built in East Boothday. 1967.* E. L. Boutilier. (Courtesy of the *Boothbay Register*)

"That was where I had my first beer," one said.

"It was a *big* deal," another recalled. "We got the day off school."

T'Donald closed their restaurant on Memorial Day to give his staff a breather. The Thistle Inn had catered five banquets in two weeks.

Leonie and T'Donald cleaned up on All Hallows Eve, because their inn was the only licensed joint open for miles and a ticket was twenty-five cents. They served 'steak on a broomstick' and a 'witch's brew'. Beverages were either 50 cents or one dollar. Pumpkins decorated the porch and customers vied to pin a paper tail on a cardboard donkey. Other patrons bobbed for apples in the pub, one galvanized washtub was full of vodka. Prizes were given out for most imaginative and funniest costumes. A hearse pulled up in the Thistle's parking lot. A casket lid creaked open and out came a white-faced corpse in a black suit who walked into the pub and ordered a drink.

T'Donald died of a heart attack on November 21st, 1967. He was forty-one.

Staff rallied around Leonie. She placed a notice in the *Boothbay Register* a few days later. "Thank you for all your kindness and thoughtfulness - and particular gratitude to our wonderful staff who made it possible for the Inn to carry on after T'Donald died." Leonie wished everyone a wonderful Thanksgiving and advertised a roast beef - lobster seafood Newburg buffet on Saturday nights. "As T'Donald would have wanted it, business as usual."

Leonie went to Simmons' Funeral Home for a coffin. She brought the brochure to the pub and asked customers to help select one.

LEONIE PICKS UP THE REINS (1968-1981)

Leonie moved downstairs to room one after her husband died, easier than living with memories upstairs. She put a desk in the living room opposite room one and used that space as an office. If anyone tried to come in, Leonie drove them out.

The following year, Leonie added a tribute to T'Donald on the Thistle's menu cover.

Donald Booth Morren

Born in Edinburgh, Scotland, T'Donald Morren, founder and Chef of the Inn died suddenly on November 21, 1967. He left a legacy of wonderful recipes, an unusually well-stocked wine cellar and his delightful spirit which is still reflected in the atmosphere of the Inn. His widow, Leonie, is carrying on in the tradition he created and hopes everyone will enjoy it as he would have wished.

Several offers were made to buy the Thistle Inn. Leonie turned them all down. She wanted to keep the inn for a year out of respect for her husband. Her commitment lasted fourteen years.

She eventually moved back to the top-level of the house and room one, the best at the inn, was let out to guests.

Strohn Woodard recalled the summer he married. The reception was at the Thistle Inn. "My parents came for my wedding and stayed at the Thistle. My father said, 'If I'd have known New England Inns were like this I'd have stayed in all of them.' There was a refrigerator in room one (Leonie's old room) and my father put a case of Budweiser in there and was in heaven."

The Thistle Inn sponsored a Drunken Sailors' Race. Contestants had to compete in a sailboat with a beautiful woman onboard. Meetings to update regulations for this outrageous summer event were held during winter in the pub, with Leonie's blessing. Rules for alcohol consumption changed from year to year. Originally a case of beer or a flagon of wine had to be drunk by the end of the race. One time they decorated marker buoys with bottles of liquor, picked up as sailors passed.

"It could never happen today," a fisherman's wife said. "Oh geez no. Wasn't it fun though?"

All types of vessels entered that crazy competition, bathtubs with improvised sails and once a fishing boat towed Leonie in a canoe. The Thistle's raft won by default one year because the winner, André Warren's *Y Worry*, sailed away and André forgot to collect the award. But a trophy was never a main objective and those who finished last were given an honorable mention.

Social norms were different in the late 1960s and ladies rarely went into a bar alone. Leonie wanted to break that pattern and encouraged single women to come in on Friday nights.

"There wasn't a girl in town that felt bad about walking into her bar," George Bourette said. "In those days, you didn't do that. Leonie told me, if people line up a date on Friday night they'll come back for dinner on Saturday. And it worked, you know."

"I'd never go in a bar on my own," a Boothbay woman said. "But the Thistle was different. I knew everyone there. It was always the local watering-hole."

Olive Stratton's rooming house was directly opposite the Thistle. Young male lodgers used Leonie's pub as their living room. George Bourette only came up to Boothbay on weekends. If he forgot to bring milk or something and the market was shut, he borrowed what he needed from the Thistle's kitchen and replaced the item the following day. "It was wonderful," George said with a wistful smile. "It was like another home."

Edee Deen met her future husband, Bruce, a scallop diver, at the Dory Bar. "Somebody tried to pick me up," she said. "And Bruce gallantly stood up and said, 'She's with me.'"

When Rocky Lewis came back from the Vietnam War, he worked as a mailman by day and played honkytonk on the Thistle's piano after he finished his deliveries. He was a great crowd-pleaser and enjoyed generous tips, beer and sandwiches. Leonie hired Rocky and his Travellons to play at dances that started at 9 p.m. Cover charge was a dollar. "In the meantime try practicing dancing in an area about the size of a fifty cent piece," Leonie said, "as I think it may be a wee bit crowded." Rocky's music appealed to all ages and Leonie claimed that a generation gap disappeared when he played the piano.

Kay Brown also performed at the Thistle. As a child, her mother had taken her to minstrel shows at the Boothbay Harbor Opera House and her grandmother owned a piano and stacks of sheet music. "So all that type of thing was in my head," Kay said. "I was taking classical lessons so I could memorize quickly. You were in an environment where people wanted to sing along and it was casual. There was no hiring at that time, it was just fun. And anybody that wanted a song I'd say, 'Well let's see,' and we'd do that."

Leonie did pay Kay as time went on. "It was just one of the most exciting times in my life, to have that place to go to," Kay said. "And Leonie was a character."

The Thistle's head bartender, Bobby Rice, was a classmate of Kay's. He always requested, 'Tico-Tico', a Brazilian choro number. Bobby, a stocky guy with a boyish smile, often impersonated W. C. Fields in *My Little Chickadee*. To many of the Thistle's patrons, Bobby sounded more authentic than Fields. Bobby sometimes had a 'buck night', when everything except specialty drinks was one dollar.

David Norton told a story about how he came to Boothbay Harbor in 1970.

He was in the Merchant Marine. On one trip he tore his finger and when they reached Baltimore his captain gave him six weeks off with subsistence pay. David spent a few days with his family in Camden, Maine, then set off for Colorado. Vail, a mountaintop resort, had taken off and David planned to work there that summer. On his way David stopped in Boothbay Harbor to catch up with his shipmate, Bobby Lee, to whom David owed twenty bucks.

"Well we oughta have a drink before yer go," Bobby said.

"You can't get a drink in Maine at nine o'clock in the morning."

"Oh no, I know the bartender at the Thistle," Bobby said. (The inn was open for breakfast.) "We'll go down to the Thistle."

Two weeks later David was still in Boothbay Harbor. He eventually said goodbye to his new friends at the Thistle and left for Colorado. He was on the Portsmouth traffic circle in New Hampshire and wondered why he was leaving. Boothbay Harbor was fantastic. David passed a southbound exit, swung onto a northbound lane and headed back to Maine.

"What are you doing here?" his pals said when he walked in the Thistle.

"I think I'm gonna stay for the summer."

David Norton never went to Colorado. He took a job at the Thistle. "That night Leonie said to me, 'Now you can drink while you tend bar, but if you get into the champagne please drink the cheap stuff first.' " The more expensive brands were at the bottom of the cooler.

The Thistle was always boisterous on Wednesday nights, because a women's bowling league knocked back booze after they knocked down candlepins at Romar Lanes. One time the Boothbay bowlers arrived with a competing team. They kept David so busy he forgot to check the time. He finally glanced at the clock by the piano. He had intended to close at midnight but now it was two:

LAST CALL!

Customers drove home in someone else's vehicle if theirs was blocked in the Thistle's parking lot, people left keys in the ignitions. Sometimes cars were three deep. A lawyer from Bath took David Norton's '68 GTO and left his new station wagon hitched to a Boston Whaler. Several days went by before the Bath guy returned. David never complained. During the week he and a buddy had taken the boat for a joyride off Ocean Point.

Leonie's place cast a spell. David Norton met a local girl at the Thistle Inn, married her and settled in Boothbay. Rusty Court had told his version of David's proposal to Sanny (Suzanne) in the Thistle and the Nortons wanted to set me straight. Lobster traps were stacked in their backyard and I took in a view of Back River as I stamped my boots to shake off snow. The air was brisk and bright, a perfect winter's day.

I settled on their couch. David weighed in. "One night Bobby Rice was tending bar and Minzy was sitting there with a drink and said,

'Bobby, you and Anita ought to get married 'cause I've got a new sports coat and I'd like to wear it some place.'

"Bobby just laughed and said, 'David's here; go ask David, he'll do it.'

"And Minzy came up to me and said, 'Listen, why don't you and Sanny get engaged?'

"I said, 'Great idea.' So I went right over and said, 'Why don't we get married?'

"So she said, 'Yes.'"

Fishermen can be blunt, no romantic fluff, but Sanny smiled at him in that intimate way people have who have lived together for years. David continued, his words interspersed with his distinctive chuckle. "So then later that night, on the pay phone at the Thistle, Sanny called her parents and her father answered. She said, 'David and I are gonna to get married.' And he said, 'Call me back in the morning, you've had too much to drink.' They were teetotalers and that was how that went."

Buddies from the Thistle Inn attended their wedding and Minzy wore his new Harris Tweed jacket. The bride's parents and grandmother hosted a buffet at their home. As they abstained from alcohol only a bowl of Hawaiian punch was offered. "Bobby Rice, of course, laced it with vodka," Sanny said. "We were only there for a little while and then we went to Cliffy's house and had the real reception."

A bizarre wedding ceremony took place in the Thistle's pub one weekday afternoon. A former financier—ribbed often enough about his love affair with Five O' Clock Vodka—formally married a bottle in front of sixty guests. The groom's favorite barmaid, Karen Perkins, played along and acted as best man.

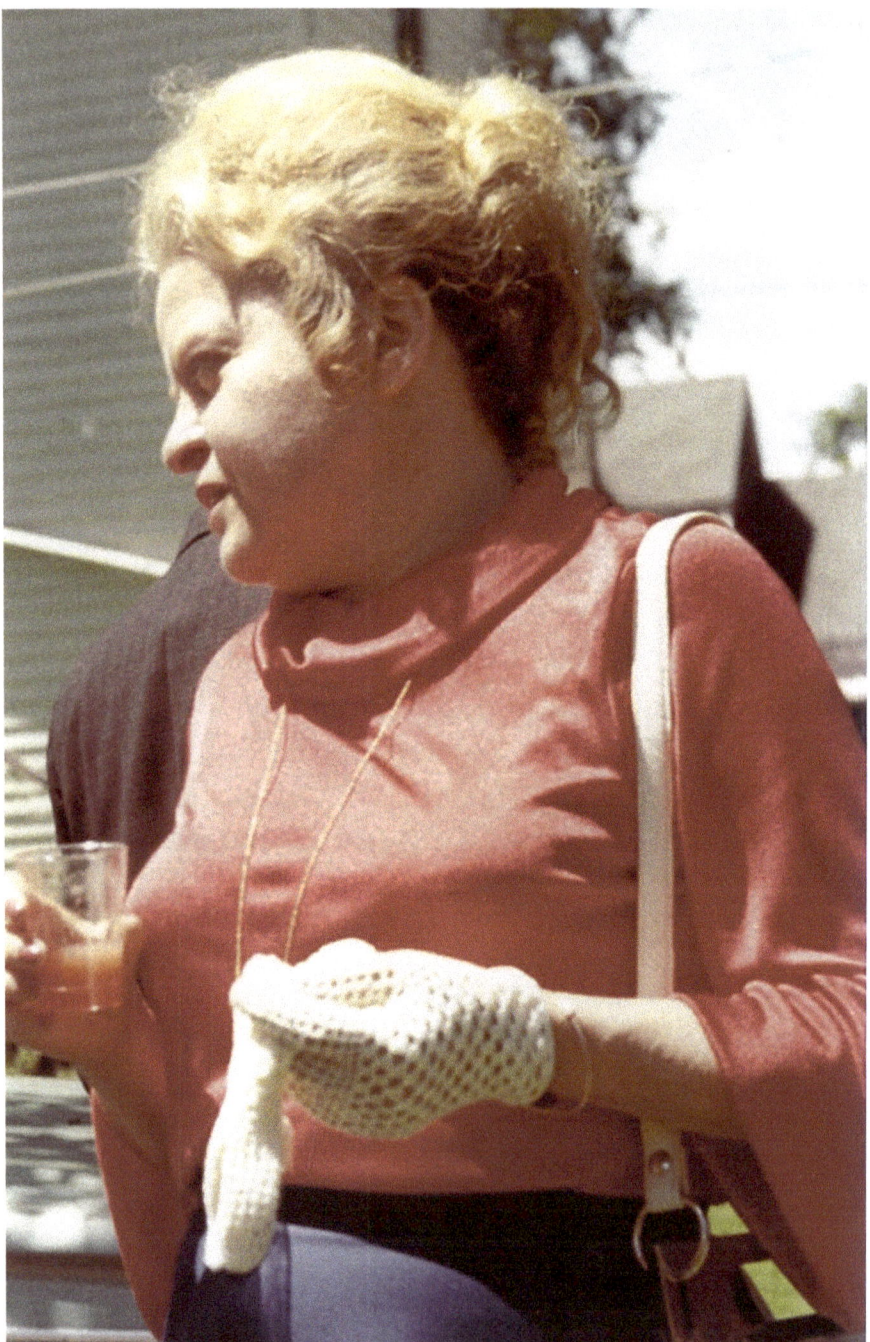

Leonie at the Nortons' wedding. 1971. (Courtesy of Sanny Norton)

Leonie sometimes had to contend with firearms. One irate fisherman brought his rifle into the pub. He claimed his wife, a waitress, had been too friendly with a male customer. Leonie confiscated the husband's gun and locked the weapon in her living room.

Later on, two warring families on Back Narrows Road carried their feud into the Thistle one night. Rumor was that Leonie brought the rifle in the pub and pointed it at them. A bartender called the cops while Leonie faced them down. A squad car drew up, but both officers stayed in the vehicle.

Leonie marched out. "Okay, you can come in, it's safe now."

She could handle anybody. One time she made a citizen's arrest. If a customer misbehaved Leonie said, "If I throw you out of here where are you going to go? So you better shut up right now." The Thistle Inn was the only bar open in town in winter.

A former pot washer said, "My feeling about her was that she pretty much understood how men work. Most of those guys in there, if anything ever happened they would protect her. You didn't give her any shit or somebody would beat the crap out of you."

Several items were nonetheless swiped from the inn, including an antique high chair on loan from a friend and a picture of a Highlander with a plaid slung over one shoulder. One day the frame was empty but for a note written by Leonie, "Here was once a fine painting of a Scotsman that was stolen." A few pieces were returned after she pleaded in the *Boothbay Register*. But then vandalism broke out. Leonie banged a glass down on the bar counter. Her begonias had been trampled and her window boxes smashed. "From now on, if you wish to see seasonal decorations you'll just have to step *inside* our Inn," she said in a subsequent notice to the newspaper.

She needed someone to share the burden.

She married Jim Fitch.

The ceremony was at All Saints by-the-Sea on Southport Island, the reception was at the Thistle. She moved out of her living quarters at the inn into Jim's seaside cottage on Southport.

Jim was a tall and stout contractor. Someone asked him if he was the owner of the Thistle Inn. "Yeah," Jim said. "Not bad for a fifteen dollar investment, huh?" $15 was the cost of a marriage license in the seventies. Jim loved his new wife but hated her hounds. Tattle at the bar was that he sat at their waterfront cottage and swatted the dogs when Leonie was down at the Thistle.

Rumors flew round Leonie's tavern like gulls after bait. Steamy stories circulated about furtive meetings on the second floor. Sometimes scuttlebutt about townsfolk was confirmed in the local newspaper. You needed to be on good terms with your ex. You were bound to run into him or her at the Thistle with a new date.

Leonie hired Phil Koskela as head chef. Phil, a quiet well-mannered fellow, had just finished culinary school and hotel management. He slaved in the Thistle's kitchen over breakfast, lunch and dinner. Two older waitresses, Millie Giles and Dorothy Dewitt, took pity on Phil and brought him a cocktail after he finished at night. Phil used his own flair with specials, but Leonie insisted that he follow the Thistle's recipes. She wanted everything on the menu to be exactly the same as when T'Donald was alive.

T'Donald's Scottish Sherry Trifle

Bavarian cream
Raspberries
Ladies Finger biscuits
Cream sherry
Whipped cream

- Break Lady Fingers into pieces and place at the bottom of sundae glasses. Top with raspberries. Douse liberally with sherry. Cover with a layer of Bavarian cream.

- Repeat layers until glasses are almost full. Leave overnight to soak up sherry.

- Top with whipped cream, then serve.

Phil lived at Leonie's Southport cottage that summer. "Leonie loved everybody," he said. "She'd do anything for anybody." Leonie's moods, however, shifted as fast as Maine's weather. Just for kicks, she twisted Phil's hair until he almost cried. "She'd come out in the kitchen when it got really busy," Phil said. "And there'd be just me and a dishwasher; that was it. She would scream at me, 'People have been waiting!' And I'd say, 'Leonie I'm here by myself all summer long.' I did not grow up and go to school with people quite like her. So she was an eye-opener for me. In the fall, when things quieted down, she closed the place one weekend and invited her first two husbands to stay."

A staircase led from the ground floor living room up to room five, where Phil lived that winter. One night he invited a few fellows over, music was loud. Leonie's voice boomed from downstairs, "PHIL! You get down here NOW."

His pals scrambled out of a window and jumped off the porch roof to avoid Leonie. Phil went down to get reamed out.

Maine's legal drinking age was reduced from twenty-one to eighteen in 1972. A State liquor identification card was available from Augusta for a dollar. "Because of faked birth certificates and drivers' licenses that have been handed around, such precautions are necessary," Leonie said in one of her ads.

The Thistle's pub was mobbed every night. Phil Koskela recalled the year that teenagers were allowed in the Thistle's pub. "Boy, the fishermen were upset. That was a fisherman's bar." Leonie asked Phil to bounce on the door at night after he finished in the kitchen. A friend of his covered the porch door. "We had to stop people coming in," Phil said. "And, boy, when you tell a fisherman he can't come into the bar! I'm a twenty-one-year-old who had never had a fight in my life. It was an interesting situation."

Youngsters spent summer on the Thistle's porch to avoid taunts from fishermen in the pub. Bruce Burnham, owner of Boothbay Boat Sales, reminisced about the first year he went to the Thistle. "Part of it was I was local and some of the fishing crowd were a bit over the top for me as a young guy. My mother was never a bar-goer, but she enjoyed going up to the Thistle because she knew all these guys and could simmer them down. And it was always an adventure, you know. Being eighteen I enjoyed the older ladies there. A very attractive group of women went to the Thistle. They flirted with me. I thought that was great."

One of Bruce's favorite memories was of a hot July night. At last call somebody on the porch said, "Why don't we go skinny-dipping in West Harbor Pond?" (A local swimming hole.) Word spread through the pub like wild fire. "Truthfully, forty people left the Thistle Inn," Bruce said. Fun turned to dismay when cops showed up in a cruiser at the pond, switched on their high beams and freaked out a bunch of naked girls.

Problems arose after teenagers were allowed to drink at the Thistle Inn. Leonie dealt a swift blow by way of the newspaper.

THE THISTLE INN
OPEN ALL YEAR
Mother, Oh Mother, where is thy son?
The clock in the steeple strikes one.

As you probably read in this ad we commend the young people on their behavior this summer under the new legal age for consuming alcoholic beverages. However, it is winter now and there seems to be some confusion in thinking the new law makes an innkeeper a substitute parent. If they have learned no respect for other people's property, or other people and do not know how to comport themselves, they will not be welcome here. We have instituted a barred list and a probation list and they will be strictly enforced. When necessary, parents will be contacted, although with the new legal age laws their hands are tied in many areas.

Perhaps if we all cooperate a serious problem can be nipped in the bud.
P.S. We've got lists for the over 21s too!

Records were pinned up behind the bar. A name was scratched out only if they showed remorse and changed their behavior.

Leonie was seated on a stool at the Dory Bar with a copy of the *Boothbay Register* in her hand, when a young man came in and ordered a beer. He had almost drunk half when she dropped her newspaper on the counter and pointed at him. "You, OUT, now!" she said. His name was in the 'Police Blotter' for a speeding ticket along with his age; too young to drink alcohol in her pub.

She was more lenient with Merritt Grover when he was underage. He had worked in his family's hardware business since he was ten. "So I got to know Leonie quite well," Merritt said, "from waiting on her in the store. Leonie was quite fond of me." He joked that he could name the most popular barrooms by how often they needed toilet parts. Merritt was eager to check out the 'happening place' in town. He and a buddy passed the Thistle Inn one rowdy night and snuck in via the porch door. Merritt was seated on a step at a fringe of a mob bellied up to the bar when Leonie nabbed him.

"Merritt Grover, what are you doing here?"

Merritt squirmed. Leonie chuckled and bought him a beer before kicking him out.

Maude Wright, a fisherman's wife, fondly recalled her youth at the Thistle. I gazed at a pen and ink sketch of the *Sea Bring* shrimp boat in her living room as she spoke. "I've got to tell you, the seventies were the best years I've lived here. You couldn't find a chair. You remember the summer? Because I remember always drivin' up to find a parkin' place and everybody's hangin' outside on that back porch. We just loved it. They called me a summer-jerk every day of my life," Maude said, even though she moved here year-round and went to Boothbay Region High

School. "The Squirrels [kids from Squirrel Island] and all the Southport people met goin' to town. But we all had boats and just knew everybody when we started workin', waitressin' together and we're all doin' the Thistle."

Ice-cold drinks were taken out to the porch on hot sultry nights. Customers sat on rockers or white slatted chairs. "If there is a breeze anywhere, you'll find it on our porch," Leonie advertised. When there was a crowd, they spilled onto the Thistle's front lawn. Boothbay Harbor's police chief cruised by and if that outside gang was too rowdy he phoned Leonie to tell her to rein in her customers.

Patricia Royall, a local gal, added, "It wasn't just the young crowd at the Thistle. There was an older group too, people's parents went."

Leonie experimented to stay afloat in the winter of 1972. Phil Koskela toiled in the kitchen. Oriental meals were available on Sundays. The Thistle Inn restored a policy to cater parties from twenty-five to two hundred and fifty people.

"Two of you could go out for a whole evening at the Thistle and eat and drink for less than ten bucks," a fisherman's wife recalled.

Cheap luncheon specials were advertised.

A neighbor of mine, Nancy Gaecklin, worked at the Thistle Inn when she was younger. She recalled early mornings in the pub. "We were always there at that big table and there'd be six, eight, ten of us hanging out having coffee and Leonie would say, 'We're not open yet.'"

Nancy bartended on weekends to make money for nursing school. Her nerves were strung out like washing lines as the deadline approached, short for her tuition.

"You're going to be there Monday morning," Leonie said to her. "Even if I have to write a check myself."

THE THISTLE INN

OPEN ALL YEAR

Because of the interest shown in our Specials, we are listing below the prices and what our luncheon specials will be on a specific day next week.

Monday – Liver and onions	$1.50
Tuesday – Homemade Pea Soup and Corn Bread	$1.00
Wednesday – New England Boiled Dinner	$1.75
Thursday – Pot Roast	$1.75
Friday – Broiled or Fried Fresh Fish	$1.75
Saturday – Fried Chicken	$1.50
Sunday – Roast Beef and Ham Sandwiches	$1.00

12 noon 'til 9:00 p.m.

Nancy graduated in 1973 and Leonie applauded her in the *Boothbay Register*. "It is with heartfelt pleasure and pride that we announce that one of the mainstays of the Thistle Inn over the last nine years (Chambermaid, Waitress, Errand Girl etc.), Nancy Hasson Dansbury, had the fortitude to attend S.M.V.T.I. (Maine School of Practical Nursing) for the past year and is graduating as a Licensed Practical Nurse this week. With two children to care for and a daily drive to the Portland area she is commended especially for her independence under difficult circumstances. Welfare was not her way out! Bravo Nancy! We are proud of you."

"I loved Leonie, she was like a mentor," Nancy said. "She was very generous." Nancy and her children lived in a cramped apartment in town. When it was hot, Leonie invited them to stay at her seaside cottage on Southport, where it was cooler. (Leonie lived there with her husband.) Nancy remarried a few years later. "Leonie threw us a reception at the inn. There was an open bar and rooms for all our guests."

"Everyone has been price conscious recently and we have tried to keep our prices as reasonable as possible," Leonie said in the *Boothbay Register* in spring of 1973. "However, because of the high quality of our meat and the portions served, we had to go up slightly, 10 cents on hamburgers for instance."

For nine years the Thistle Inn was the only fully licensed year-round restaurant in Boothbay Harbor. Then later that year (1973), two competitors announced their intention to stay open in winter. Leonie felt a pinch. She kept the pub open but shut down the restaurant in fall and reversed the Thistle's policy to serve only fresh food. Premade snacks were available at the Dory Bar. Servers cooked them in a Stewart, infrared, sandwich oven. Canadian burgers and pastrami sandwiches were a hit. They ran out of them in four days. Ham and cheese, sloppy joes and chuck wagon style burgers were also popular. Leonie kept this snack option through summer and they could be ordered in the pub after dining rooms closed.

Walter and Connie Manter, from Groton, Massachusetts, bought a piece of land on Farnham Point in East Boothbay. They planned to build a house and stayed in a friend's cottage with one light bulb, one radio, one outhouse and two kids.

"We didn't have any heat down there, we had a fireplace that's it, not even a woodstove," Connie said. "We came in the summer and on weekends in the fall and spring. And you know what spring is like, it's still cold and the Thistle was still warm. So our place of respite was the Thistle. There was a nice bathroom, it was small but we loved it, it was a *real* bathroom. We sat in the corner in the bar and Bobby Rice gave the kids twelve cherries and two cokes and us a good strong drink. The kids were like two and three. I can remember being there because it was warm and they welcomed us. They didn't mind doing a hamburger for all of us, for we didn't have much money. So our memories are really kind of colorful, because we'd keep going year after year. It took us several years to build. The Thistle was our survival place, but also our fun place, because it was where we got to know a lot of people."

Local fishermen organized an annual event to generate funds for a memorial to honor men who had died at sea. Leonie pitched in on behalf of Boothbay Region Chamber of Commerce. The first, in March 1974, was called the Lincoln County Shrimp Festival. Rusty Court was in the tug o' war. "We got beat up pretty bad. The Boothbay boys had a big heavy team and we only had twelve fishermen on Monhegan. They had a lot to pick from and it didn't matter if they were fishermen or they pulled them out of the shipyard or whatever, they had some *big* boys."

After shrimp stocks crashed and failed to revive it became the Fishermen's Festival. Boatloads of islanders headed to the Thistle Inn to stay for weekend festivities. Leonie sold tickets at the Dory Bar for a cabaret dance at Boothbay Harbor's Opera House. "In honor of Fishermen's Festival we will be serving our Special, Shrimp Creole, as only our Chef Brock can cook it," Leonie advertised. "Also for the thirsty wayfarers we will serve a Fishermen's Special at the Dory Bar. So drop in between the many interesting events."

The festival kicked off with an evening talent pageant to be Miss Shrimp Princess and wear a silver crown. Crowds cheered from a pier on Saturday morning when fishermen zipped around the harbor to haul, bait and set lobster traps in record time. Kids ran along a line of crates tied to a dock. Teams of teenagers belted along Commercial Street in foul-weather gear and passed a slimy codfish from hand to hand in a relay race. In the afternoon contestants mended nets, filleted redfish and shucked clams or scallops before packed bleachers in the high school gym.

Area clergymen blessed the fleet on Sunday at a dock on the east side; fishing boats lined up and almost stretched to the horizon. A priest read out names of local men who had died at sea with a date and brief description of the circumstances. The record goes back to 1798 and includes Captain Samuel Miller Reed lost with his ship in 1863, whose house became the Thistle Inn.

Tall Tales followed at the Thistle. Everyone piled in the pub. "Our idea was to encourage older men to spin yarns about their seagoing adventures," said Rusty Court, an organizer. "Or to pin a little something on your neighbor, and then your neighbor got up and said, 'That wasn't really the way it went, you know.'"

Dean Morrison, a sternman on Douglas Carter's fishing boat, had a room at the Thistle. "That damn Carter," Dean said in an interview for the *Boothbay Register*, "once worked on Leonie to get me into the trap haulin' contest. I didn't want no part of it. But Carter stayed after her, you know what I mean, [flattery worked on Leonie]. So I signed up. But I got even with Carter at the bar one night – shamed him into doing the Fishermen's Festival Tall Tales. He was great!"

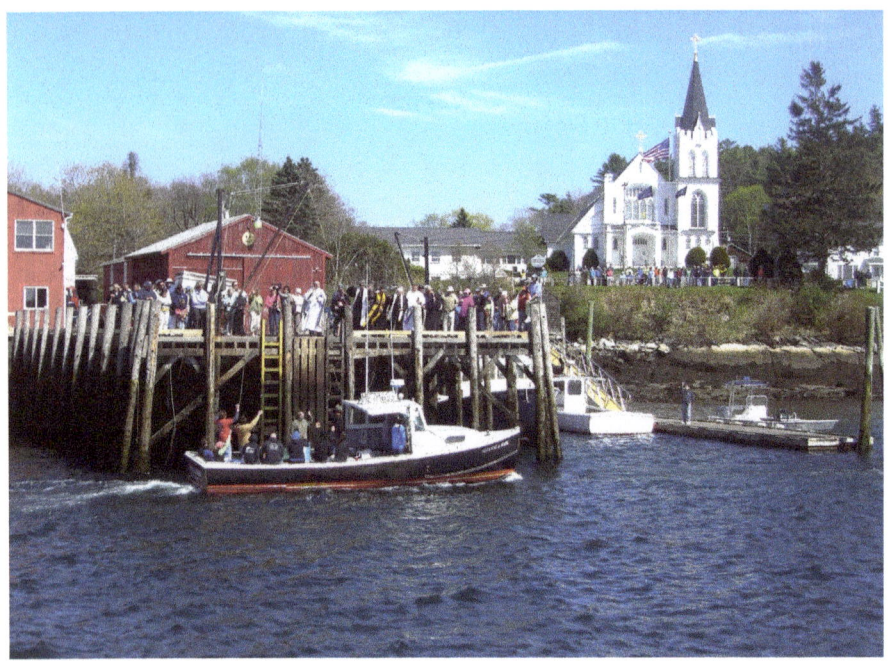

Blessing of the Fleet on the east side of the harbor (Catholic Church in background). 2000. Hilary E. Bartlett

Douglas Carter made up a story about purse seining which captures schools of fish. His dories were in town. He was off Damariscove Island. Douglas had told his sternman that if he found any fish he would fire off a couple of flares to signal he wanted his dories taken to the cove. Douglas fired off his flare gun when he found a shoal of herring. Someone onshore reported a vessel was in distress. A helicopter came up from Portland and a Coast Guard boat went out from Boothbay Harbor. Meanwhile Douglas returned with his catch.

His audience roared their approval. Douglas won a trophy, a dory on top of a piece of mahogany. Awards were also given out for newest and oldest wooden boat, best dressed fisherman and ugliest pick-up truck in town.

In the ten years since the Thistle Inn opened, they had installed a pay phone and a cigarette machine. Wooden stools and tables were carved with initials and dates. More bric-a-brac adorned the walls, like the poster for a bullfight in Spain, or the painting of a man leaning to one side with a tilted building in the background. That piece of art, painted from a drunkard's perspective, always made newcomers chuckle. A life-ring from Cuckolds Island Lighthouse (five miles south of the Thistle) hung in a booth. Wisecracks were made at those who sat underneath.

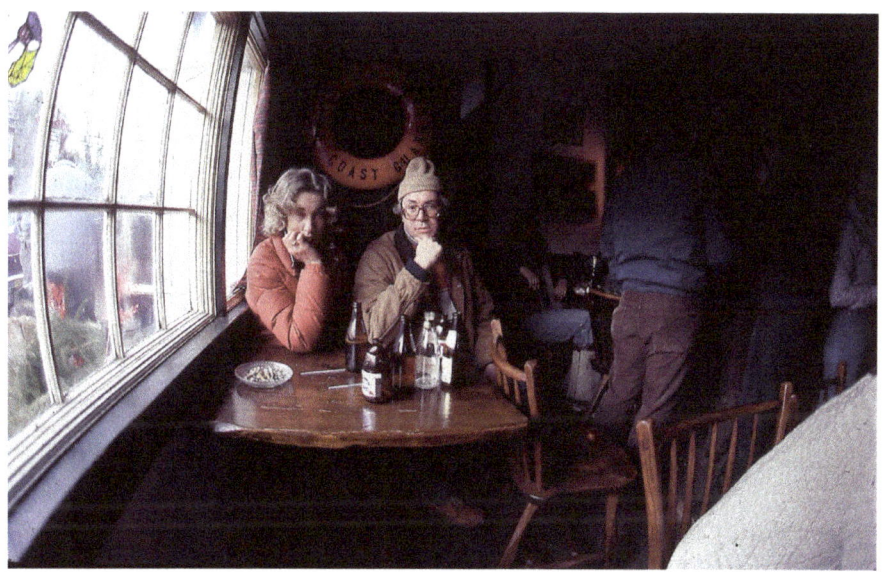

Cuckolds life ring near front entrance of the Thistle's pub. Edee Deen and Jim Fowler at the table. 1970s. Stephen Rubicam.

Candles at both ends of the Dory Bar were stuffed into bottles covered with multicolored layers of dried on wax. "They were gross," Sanny Norton said. "Think of all the dust and cigarette smoke embedded in that tallow." They took on a slimy appearance on humid evenings. Leonie, however, was attached to them and went berserk when one was stolen and the other was damaged by careless handling. The Thistle Inn was almost lost because of those stupid candles. Someone forgot to snuff them out when they closed the bar one night. A guest in room one smelled smoke and called the fire brigade.

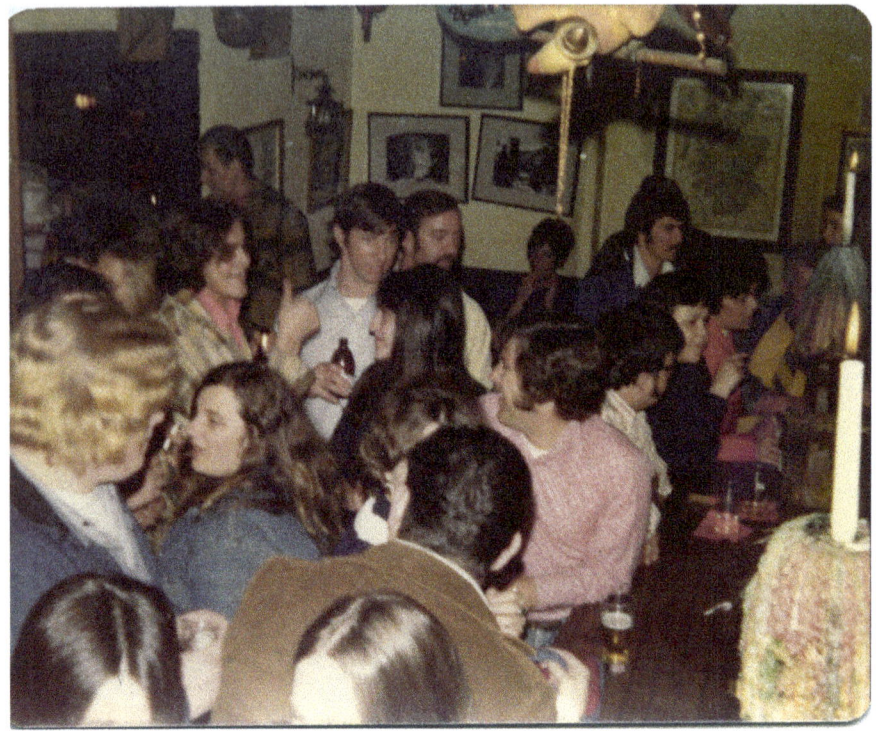

The infamous candles in the pub. 1974. Patricia Irish.

Leonie was able to keep a full restaurant service open in winter 1974, thanks in part to Bigelow Laboratory for Ocean Sciences that opened the previous summer. Their scientists ate in her dining rooms and drank in her pub. The new research institution was the brainchild of Charlie Yentsch, and it was named for his hero Henry Bigelow, famed for research in the Gulf of Maine. Buildings were rented from Maine's Department of Marine Resources (D.M.R.) on McKown Point in West Boothbay Harbor.

In January a Bigelow vessel disappeared with five people on board. They had set out from Boothbay Harbor for a four-day research cruise, calm conditions forecast. Several scientists waited for hours at the Thistle for the crew to return.

Betsy Bass recalled that harrowing night at the Dory Bar. "We'd left it that when they came back we were going to get scallops and cook them at the Welch House [a communal property near Bigelow Lab]. And they didn't come in and they didn't come in. Then we were told that there had been a Mayday. Everything is a blur after that because we started the search process and were waiting."

The Coast Guard failed to make radio contact. In spite of an extensive air and sea search, only one body was retrieved in waters off Jeffrey's Ledge, sixty-three miles south west of Boothbay Harbor. The boat had been in excellent condition and unexplained sightings and theories abounded. The mystery has never been solved.

Leonie organized a series of events in dreary winter months after New Year, 1975. She loved to kick up her heels, especially on the Dory Bar. Her legs had been featured in a Pan Am commercial.

Her talent night was based on TV's *Gong Show*. The fee was one dollar or else you brought back a glass taken from the Thistle. Customers sang, danced, or did comic routines. "Knock 'em dead," a fellow called to cheer on his mate. Some contestants were swiftly dispatched. Leonie was MC.

Her next event was a Fairy Ball. Leonie in a spangled dress strode down the bar top in high heels. "Fairy dust for you and for you," she said with a serious face as she tapped customers' shoulders with a silver wand and sprinkled them with glitter. And when she came to a gay guy she said, "And *a lot* for you."

A streaking fad—running naked through a public place—was raging through America with sightings at a Super Bowl, the Academy Awards and political events. Leonie advertised a Thistle Streakers' Ball with mandatory ties and sneakers. Her inn was jammed with expectant onlookers. Things swiftly degenerated when Douglas Carter captured a naked contestant and sat him on a stool by the cash register. "Stick around and I'll buy yer one," Douglas said and would not let him move.

Leonie held a Depression Ball. "Recession, move over . . . we know a depression when we feel it," she said in a newspaper ad. "So pick your worn clothing, get in the breadline, enjoy a scant apple and get served two glasses with each beer. In the meantime try to keep the meagre cash flow by dropping by for the best drink in Maine for the most reasonable price; cokes and Shirley Temple's still twenty-five cents."

Fritzie and Friedel, the two cats, moved into Leonie's Southport cottage after her fourth husband, Jim Fitch, moved out. Leonie held a Grand Controversial Divorce Ball. Happily married couples were encouraged to attend and provide a more well-balanced point of view. "Rocky will be merrily playing away with his cohorts," Leonie advertised. "And we entreat everyone to give some thought to a different costume. For a start, mine will be decorated with dollar bills – Women's Lib, ho, ho, ho." The door prize was a free marriage license for the person with the most divorces. Leonie won that. Her track record for ex-husbands rivaled Liz Taylor's.

Jeff Savastano and his wife, Adele, are current owners of Slick's boutique in Boothbay Harbor and in the spring of 1975 Jeff played music at the Thistle with Paula Hartford and her sister, Ruthie. "Paula Hartford is nowadays known as Chapin Hartford," Jeff said at his Victorian farmhouse in East Boothbay. "That was her middle name and she took that when she went to Nashville. She became a very successful Grammy-nominated songwriter. She had three or four number one hits by Alabama Country Music." 'Shake the Sugar Tree,' was another big number.

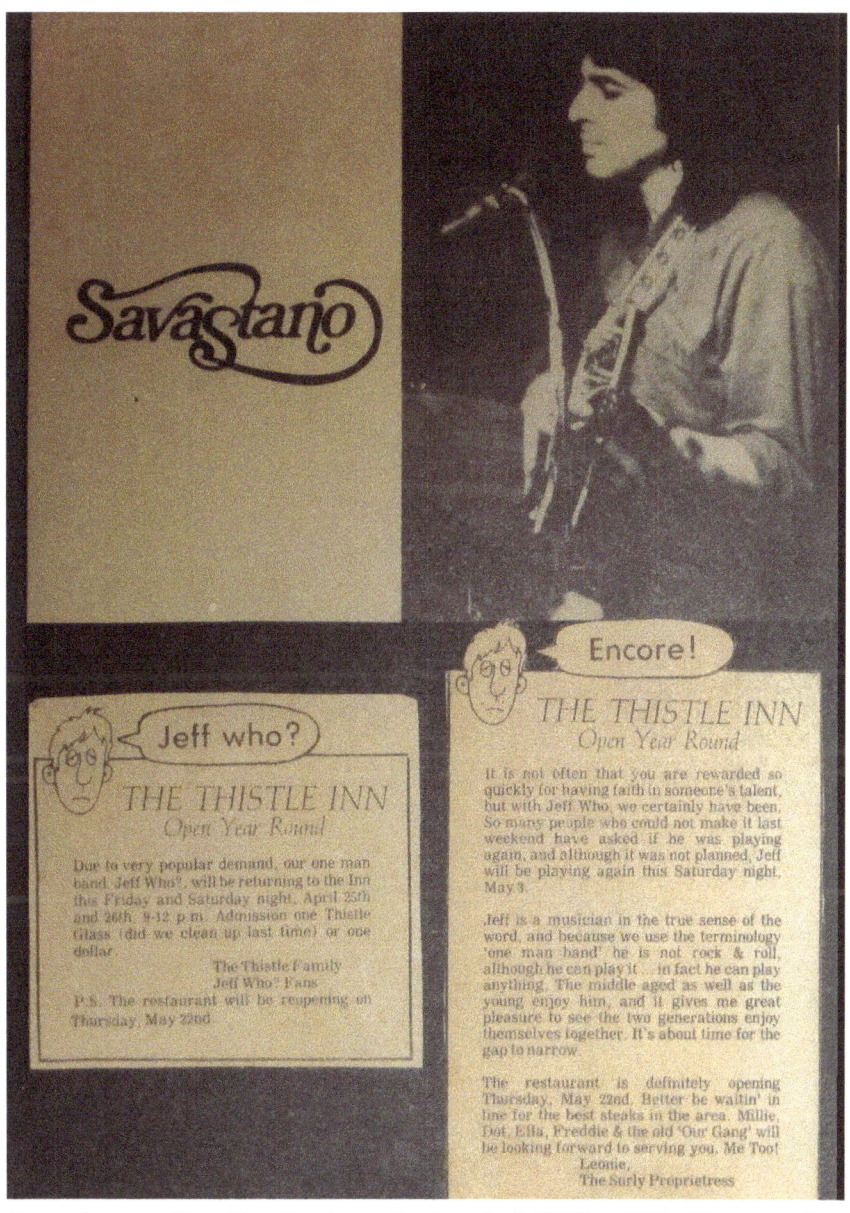

Press photo and Boothbay Register *clippings for Jeff Who. 1975.* (Courtesy of Jeff Savastano)

When Ruthie told Leonie that she and Jeff were putting an act together Leonie said, "Where can I hear that?" She came in Jeff's house and sat on a chair. He put a drum beat on and they sang a few songs. "You're singing this Friday night," Leonie said.

"We don't have enough tunes yet," Jeff said.

"Well get enough," Leonie said.

She called him Jeff Who as a joke, because of his very Italian last name, Savastano.

THE THISTLE INN

Open All Year

Just to keep spirits up until Spring finally decides to arrive to stay, we are very proud to announce that Jeff Savastano (who?) and his one man band will make his first public appearance at the Thistle Inn on the nights of April 11th and 12th. He is a very gifted and personable young man, and whether he sings or plays you will enjoy dancing to his music. You cannot help but have a musical enjoyable time. So come in between 9:00 p.m. to 12 p.m., Friday and Saturday nights April 11th and 12th and treat yourself to a real treat.

Leonie and Angus
Good music lovers

"I had a little drum machine and an electrified acoustic guitar," Jeff said. "They cleared all the tables out in the back dining room so people could dance. It was a wild crowd. I played the top forty of the day: like Crosby, Stills, Nash and Young, Blood Sweat and Tears, the Beatles. Even John Denver was huge in those days. And then the gals could sing like Bonnie Raitt and Linda Ronstadt. But a cool thing was I'd grown up in the forties and had all my parents' songs in my head. Sometimes I had fifty and sixty-year-old people in the place and I could play the Mills Brothers and Sinatra tunes, so that kept them going."

There were no wall electrical outlets in the Harness Room. Jeff had to remove a bulb from a sconce and screw in an adaptor to plug in his gear. Light show colors diffused through the smoky haze above the dancers' heads. He was in the middle of a number when his loud speaker, microphone and amplifiers cut out, - - - dadada - - - dadada - - -. The dancefloor was so full that a guy was pressed against a wall, bounced up and down and turned the switch off and on.

Jeff continued, "Leonie put in her ad the cover charge was a Thistle glass, because in those days the OUI law wasn't serious and people walked out with their drinks and went home with them. Two or three different weekends we played she got over two hundred glasses back.

"It was a rough crowd but great crowd and after a long winter people were pent-up, I guess." A serious argument flared up in front of the stage. A gal shoved her date. He pushed back and she flew through the bandstand. A boom swung across and smashed Jeff in the face. "You know how facial bleeds are," Jeff said, "and I got cut lips. I didn't get a chipped tooth but there I am singing through the blood. Talk about those Texas bars where you should be in a cage."

Another night while Jeff's band played a huge commotion broke out. Everyone fled the dance floor. A guy had streaked through the Thistle and while he was in there some joker dashed out to the flasher's car, grabbed the keys and locked his clothes inside. A crowd gathered to gawk at him buck naked in the parking lot.

THE THISTLE INN
Open Year Round

Fish scales have been scraped out for the winter. The health inspectors said OK. Lunch is being served daily from 11:30 a.m. 'til 2:00 p.m., dinner until 8 p.m. except on Fridays and Saturdays, when we're open until 9:00 p.m. Only pile drivers and similar potent potables will be served on Sundays. (Hopefully Leonie will be bringing the sandwiches.)

Leonie's Lamplighters

Rooms at the Thistle Inn were still reasonable in the seventies. Bobby Rice recalled, "When other motels were fifty or sixty dollars, the Thistle was only fifteen." Leonie's inn was fully booked in summer. In the off-season business people stayed or couples in search of a house, as well as relatives of people who lived on Monhegan Island. (The *Balmy Days* ferry took them there from Boothbay Harbor.)

A cast of characters rented rooms on a weekly basis. A husband resided at the Thistle after his wife threw him out of the house. He had once built up a successful career, but now lived above a tavern. One fellow boarded when he came home from Vietnam. He adopted a place at the Dory Bar.

His pal came in, "Aren't you ever goin' to go outside?"

"What for?" the veteran said. "I got all the fresh air I need right here," and pointed to the skylight.

One of the Thistle's lodgers came down each morning in khakis, architect's instruments in his pocket and briefcase full of plans. When the rest of Leonie's boarders left for work, he went up to his room to change clothes and spent the rest of his day at the bar. He put on work duds again before Happy Hour and raised his glass to customers when they came in. "Well," said he, "it's been a hard day."

Leonie's mother, Mrs. Adams, lived at the Thistle Inn until she moved into a nursing home. Her head barely peeked above the cash register. She bobbed up and down on her toes in order for a bartender to see her. "She probably only weighed eighty pounds wringing wet," Sanny Norton said. Mrs. Adams sipped sherry at a table next to the piano, refreshed her scarlet lipstick and painted on her eyebrows Greta Garbo style. Leonie's mother was accustomed to applying stage makeup, for she had a 1905 debut in *H.M.S. Pinafore* at the Melbourne Opera House.

The 'marine architect' and Mrs. Adams often bumped into each other at the inn. One night she was tipsy and he offered to take her up to her room. He picked her up, light as a cushion, and carried her out of the pub.

A guest noticed them on the stairs, "Be careful yer'll bang her head on the bannisters."

"Oh fuck her," said the draftsman.

Mrs. Adams's eyes shot open, "Splendid idea!"

I had my first American beer at the Thistle Inn the day after I arrived in the States on June 1st, 1975. A British agency had funded me to study tiny organisms that cause toxic red tides. Maine clam flats had been closed, health warnings issued. Ian Morris, my Ph.D. advisor at University College London, had convinced me to come to Bigelow Lab after I landed the travel fellowship. Ian was director of research and Charlie Yentsch was executive director. They took me to lunch at the Thistle. Trendy London clothes and spiky heels screamed I was 'from away' before I opened my mouth. Customers at the Dory Bar had on T-shirts and jeans with boots or sneakers. One wore waders turned down at the knees.

Ian introduced me to Bobby Rice. "Another Limey," Bobby said with a grin.

Charlie explained to me that the Thistle was a magnet for Bigelow Lab's four Brits.

"This place is brilliant," I said as I took in the old painted signs and a sailfish that leapt across the back wall. A waitress set the table with cutlery and red paper placemats. Charlie turned his over and doodled on the back to demonstrate a point about ocean color. He was a maverick, one of the first to use satellites to study the oceans.

"You should try their hamburgers," Ian said to me. "They're good here."

I frowned when I took my first bite. "It's made with beef!"

Ian Morris and Charlie Yentsch were two of Leonie's best customers. Both were heavy hitters for science funding, but never took themselves too seriously. Ian was one of Leonie's faves. Her first husband was English, her third was Scottish and she was drawn to Ian, a gregarious Welshman. He could hold his liquor. His favorite pastime was to talk science over martinis. His accent grew stronger with each one — the Welshman was a great orator. The Thistle suited him and vice versa.

Ian took on Andy Smith, a student at the University of Maine. Andy became friends with Barney Balch, Charlie Yentsch's young protégé. Andy had wheels and gave Barney rides to the Thistle.

"We didn't have a clue how important Ian and Charlie were," Barney said. "We're just summer kids having a good time. I remember Ian inviting the two of us over to lunch at the Thistle and Ian could drink anybody under the table. Then some afternoons they'd go on from lunch to dinner. I was only eighteen and never appreciated what was really going on and how big time the science was."

Scientists from around the globe visited Maine's new oceanographic lab. Academics from all over North America came to Boothbay Harbor to meet them. Bigelow Lab's directors always took visitors for a meal at the Thistle. That happened to me and changed the course of my life. Charlie Yentsch held formal dinner parties in the Mary Queen of Scots Room whenever there was a science symposium at Bigelow Lab. Cigars, speeches and brandy followed. Ian's Welsh accent grew stronger.

The Thistle Inn was an annex of Bigelow Lab. Scientific ideas were thrashed out in the pub. Paper place mats were scribbled on. Salt and pepper shakers plus ketchup bottles were used as props. Funding was tight in the lab's early days, basic equipment was scarce. I nicked an empty Schlitz bottle from the Thistle to hold a light-sensitive stain.

The Thistle Inn was like pubs back home, except for the curious, fizzy, bottled, American beer. I was used to flatter, hand-pulled, English bitter. Lee Doggett, a marine biologist, suggested we share a carafe of wine, which went down much better. American cocktails were also new. In England liquor was served straight or with a single mixer, never with ice.

Windjammer Day, in the second week in July, was such a big deal I thought it was a national holiday. No lab experiments were planned that day. We headed to the Thistle at eleven thirty and went out on the porch to watch the parade. Marching bands played, silly clowns threw candy to kids and Uncle Sam, in stars and stripes, walked about on stilts. Then Leonie rolled by in her convertible and we all stood up and cheered. The Thistle Inn had a float and shiny red firetrucks brought up the rear. After that we went down to the docks to see the windjammers come in. A gun salute rang out when a fleet of wooden schooners with streaming flags and billowing sails swept into the harbor led by the *Victory Chimes*. The navy came to celebrate too and the town was full of sailors in dress whites. Some came in the Thistle.

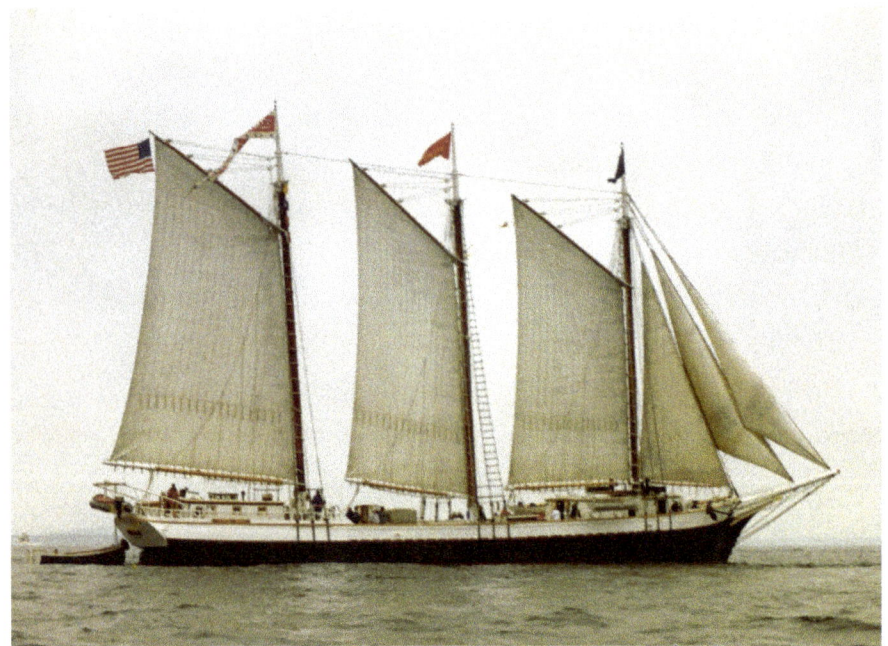

Windjammer Victory Chimes. 1994. Hilary E. Bartlett.

I was supposed to go back to England in September, but wanted to stay. I had never expected to fall in love with Boothbay Harbor, that was never part of my plan, but those three months had been some of the happiest in my life. My funding agency agreed to extend my visit by ten weeks. McKown Point authorities continued to let me bunk at the Welsh House after I offered to paint their front porch.

Charlie Yentsch suggested that I come back to work at Bigelow full time. A rental was available for the following May on Oak Street, a quaint salt-box house near Harbor Travel and opposite the Thistle. I put down a deposit. All I had to lose was a month's rent if I never returned.

My buddies threw a lunch party for me at the Thistle on my last day. I cried all the way to Portland Jetport.

I made my choice to emigrate that winter and shipped two trunks to Boston. I arrived in May 1976 with six months support on a U.K. grant, a bridge while I applied for U.S. research funding. My house was on a hill that looked down on the Thistle. The Thistle Inn looked up at the house.

Word of my return spread like an epidemic after a guy came in the pub and said, "That crazy English gal's back, I just saw her with a shoppin' cart on Oak Street. She must 'ave pushed it all the way from Finast."

More young oceanographers had joined Bigelow Lab. Frederick Durrand King was one of them. He came into the Thistle at Happy Hour, ordered a beer and joined our group.

"Hi, I'm Randy," he said to me. I bit my cheek to stifle a giggle. Randy meant horny in England.

Chris Garside, an English chemist, turned to Ian Morris and said, "Hilary came to the States to find Prince Charming and found a Randy King."

Peter Larsen, a tall blond Scandinavian at Bigelow Lab, recalled the seventies. "I bet there were ten or twelve stools and you could stand around at the prow of the boat. I can remember Fridays when it seemed like the whole town was there and you just about needed a shoehorn to get in. It took a while to get up to the bar and then it took a while for Bobby to acknowledge you."

Some patrons had a special place at the Dory Bar. Others swilled beer while their clothes dried at a laundromat. One couple sat in the Thistle too long.

Their wash disappeared.

There was a pecking order in Leonie's pub. Bigelow Lab monopolized the large back table, cribbage and card players used the one up front. Poker, five-card draw, and bid whist were popular. Dollar bills were thrown down and piled up. Sometimes they had an audience. Rhonda Selvin, a young bartender with long, flaming, red hair, played on the hearts team — rare for Boothbay Harbor, a woman on a man's team. Two other redheads worked behind the Dory Bar. They were sisters. Bobby Rice trained the three girls in the afternoon between his cribbage games. He made a customer take over at the bar if he wanted to play.

Dave Phinney, a Bigelow scientist from Freeport, Maine, described the vibe. "Man, if you ever sat round and watched those guys. I played cribbage my whole life and never felt I could sit down and play with them it was so fast. They played cut-throat, so if you didn't count your points correctly they got to take them. I was twenty-two when I first walked in there and when you have all these guys doing this stuff, you don't feel like you can really jump in the middle of it and hold your end up. I'd gone to school and was totally stoked about a job at Bigelow Lab, but it didn't take very long in the Thistle to find out I wasn't such a hot shot."

Bigelow Lab's employees were a disparate group. Locals were used to summer visitors, but they never expected a large influx of people who stayed year round. An undercurrent swirled between locals and Bigelow's scientists in the Thistle. Fishermen were suspicious of government bureaucrats and some old salts mistakenly believed we worked for Maine's D.M.R. which regulated their fishing. Others grumbled that their hard-earned tax dollars supported us and we were always in the pub. The institution actually ran on 'soft money' (grants) and each of us had to come up with new ideas. Nobody's job was safe. We let off steam at the Thistle. Over time the Bigelow crew were accepted. Leonie helped to smooth things over between the two groups. Fishermen and Bigelow's scientists were her best customers.

Terry Stockwell and his girlfriend, Lauren (now his wife), went to the Thistle every Friday night. He recalled the Thistle's old guard in the mid-seventies. "We were in the new crowd; long hair, didn't play poker – 'Goddamn hippies'. And the community was in transition then too. Whether it was folks from Bigelow Lab or people like us moving into town and in the group that we hung out with, there was a lot of summer kids who turned into year-round residents. The money-making fisheries back then weren't lobsters. It was groundfish. When I started fishing we did everything with limited access licenses. I shrimped. I dragged for fish. I dragged for scallops, dragged for groundfish. We used to go to the Fish Pier a lot and took out of Wotton's when Danny owned it. It was a slow death for the draggers. Plus the town lost its infrastructure and you had to pay. It was cheaper for the boats that were still working to land in Portland. Things started changing then too because of the two hundred mile limit that made a lot of money available. They built those longline boats down in East Boothbay and they all went to Portland because they had the infrastructure to accommodate 'em. And another interesting dynamic is the impact of drugs and how a fair amount of drugs went across the docks."

In a letter to the editor (full text, Appendix 8) Leonie outlined changes that had impacted the Thistle Inn since the mid-sixties and how difficult it was to make a profit in winter in the seventies. "Despite our loyal friends and in particular Bigelow Laboratories supporting us, we cannot afford to remain open on a full-time basis and survive." The town's income depended on boatbuilding and fishing for eight months a year, she said, and when fish stocks declined the local economy suffered. The cost of living had increased and there were fewer customers. The recent hippie-drug period had also had a negative effect. "We are certainly not perfect," said Leonie, "and like any restaurant have some bad days, but we do try to serve you the best at reasonable prices. It all really comes down to working together when the going is tough."

I was an only child, a tomboy who had only wanted brothers. Then I met the Bigelow sisters at the Thistle Inn. I ignored Ian Morris, engrossed in heavy conversation, and squished in between two of them, Susan Sykes and Linda Sapienza. All four young women worked at Bigelow but in different research groups. Several discussions buzzed around our table as glasses and beer bottles accumulated. I had been wary of girls after one had been spiteful at high school, but now I was ready to open up to these bright sparks at the Thistle. After a gal's night out with White Russians (drinks not guys), I was convinced. I went with my gut and trusted them. There was a connection. I assumed it was because they were American.

"Nah, it's special, it's different," Linda said. We fit together like pieces in a puzzle.

Susan Sykes and I carpooled to pottery classes in Brunswick. We arrived back in town just before nine, ravenous for a meal at the Thistle to celebrate Susan's birthday. The bar was full, dining rooms were empty. They had switched to winter restaurant hours, closed at eight. Both food markets had also shut. We trudged back to my place to throw a meal together. At least I had champagne in my fridge, except the cork refused to budge. A strong arm was needed. We returned to the Thistle. Bobby

Rice rolled his eyes as he opened our bottle. We blushed. Expensive bubbly helped, though my stir-fry of canned tuna fish and corn tossed with rice was a miserable substitution for the Thistle's Downeast steak.

"No one can touch our Downeast steak with its fabulous lobster sauce for $10," Leonie advertised in the newspaper. "You can miss a meal with no problem after eating one, so it's very economical." Couples split one serving until the kitchen dished out two for one on a regular basis.

Patrons tried and failed to reproduce the Thistle's Downeast sauce and Chef Brock refused to give out the recipe. A group of locals cornered him in the pub one night after his shift. They plied him with drink until he revealed his secret - a dollop of condensed mushroom soup. There was a collective gasp. They had expected the mystery ingredient to be a rare expensive commodity.

I caught up with Phil Koskela to find out more about the Thistle's renowned sauce. He was Chef before Brock. Phil recalled that the two most popular things on the menu were Downeast steak and lobster pie. The sauce was the same for both. "It was sautéed lobster with butter and sherry and Campbell's mushroom soup. That's all there was to it," Phil said.

Fisherman Billy Hallinan preferred a Robbie Burns steak, "—without all that stuff on it." He claimed that Brock was the best cook in town in the mid-seventies and remembered when he was out of commission, in hospital after a motorbike accident.

Bruce Tindal, a realtor, was a huge fan of the Thistle's Downeast steak. He and his wife were in the Harness Room with friends one night. "They're a little skimpy on the lobster," Bruce said when his surf 'n' turf arrived.

"Give me that plate," their waitress said and marched back to the kitchen.

Bruce's face lit up when she returned. His steak was smothered with seafood. "Gee thanks!" he said. "Join us for a cocktail?"

"No, no, no," she said. "Give me a minute I'll be back." A set of shelves was in the corridor that led to the kitchen. She picked up a bottle stashed behind a row of water pitchers, poured herself a drink. Bruce clinked glasses with her when she returned and gave her an extra generous tip.

The Websters owned Orne's Candy Store on Commercial Street. Their daughter, June, has wonderful memories of parties at the Thistle. "You know what we did for all our celebrations, anniversaries and family gatherings. The big deal was to have . . . what did they call it?" She paused. "It was the steak with a w-*o*-nderful lobster Newburg sauce and I believe a lobster tail or two. I make Newburg sauce and that was better than I could do. It was one of the things that really brought people there, that particular thing on the menu."

June's father sold vacuum cleaners as a sideline and delivered replacement bags for Leonie's Hoover on a regular basis. They chatted at the Dory Bar about politics, religion and the town they both loved. Theirs was a strange relationship because he was a teetotaler. He had a cup of coffee, she had a cocktail. This went on for many years. Then, when he died, his obituary was in the newspaper after the funeral.

"When Leonie read about it in the *Register* she called me on the phone in tears," June said. "She told me how much she adored my father and couldn't believe he had passed without her knowing or without her being able to pay her respects. She wanted me to tell her something she could do. And I said, 'All I could think of was just find somebody who needs a little bit of help, or a little bit of love, or a smile, and be generous with your kindness.' "

A regular upright had replaced the Thistle's old player piano. Musician, Kay Brown, frowned when she arrived in the pub one evening.

"I teased Leonie, 'Who's that guy sitting there at my piano?' "

"Danny Beal from Jonesport. Your son-in-law, Mark Stover, brought him here. They went to college in Machias. Sit down with him."

Everyone jumped when Leonie gave an order. Kay sat down with Danny.

"You play a little piano?" he said.

"Yeah, I play a little piano."

"Wanna play a song?"

"What d'you have in mind?"

"Shanty."

Kay and Danny played, '—we're gonna sit around the shanty an' get a good buzz on.' He looked at her. She looked at him. Their music clicked. That was the beginning of a wonderful friendship between Kay Brown and Danny Beal. He became Boothbay Harbor's 'Piano Man', because Billy Joel's song was Danny's signature tune.

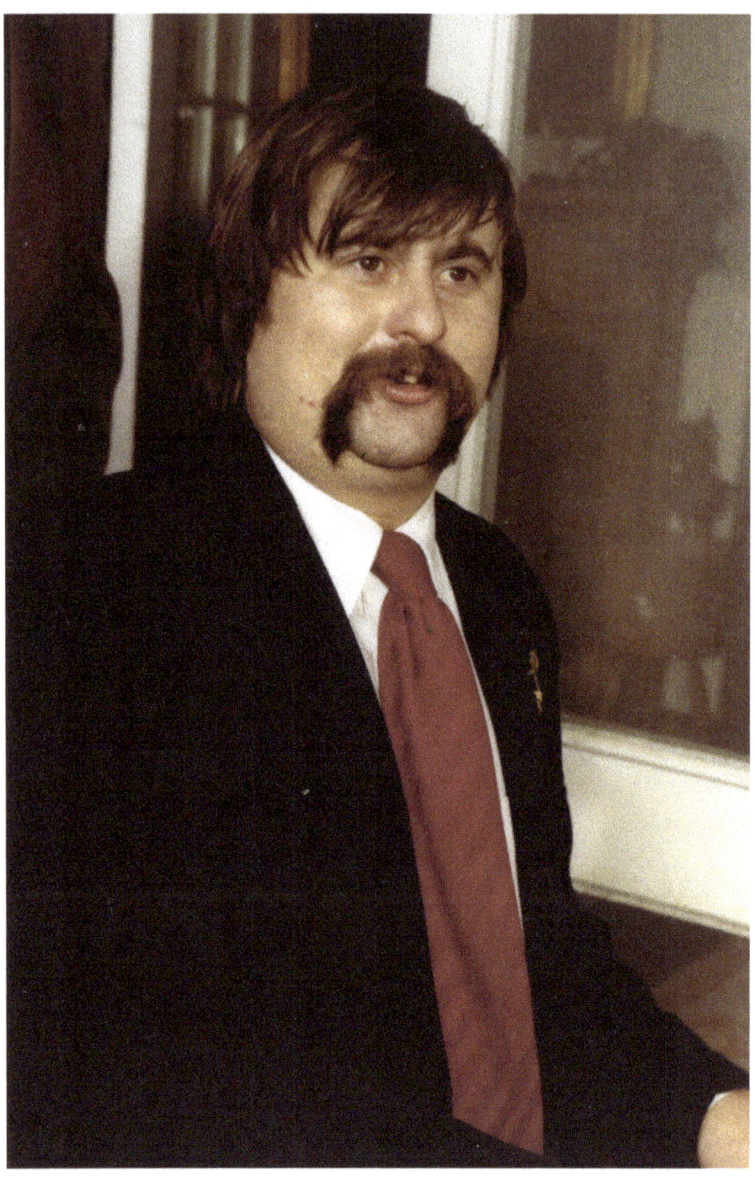

Danny Beal. 1981. Stephen Rubicam.

"Danny fit like a glove at the Thistle," said June Campbell Rose. "I remember people coming in and playing with him. Many times we'd go in and people were singing. I'll remember 'em every once in a while. But there was one song Danny played that had to do with the waitress,

Rhonda. She had beautiful red hair and she was just a wonderful waitress. But he loved that song by the Beach Boys, 'Help me Rhonda, Help - Help me, Rhonda.' Everyone chimed in and she took a bow."

"The reason I got into piano playing," Danny said, "is 'cause these really pretty women would come and sit on the bench with me and sing."

Patricia Royall, a local gal, often joined him at the piano. She had spent a year before college as a soloist with an international youth choir, 'Up with People'. Danny performed with Patricia whenever she was at the Thistle. Harmonies soared into the pub, into the dining rooms and into our hearts. Their two most requested numbers were: Neil Diamond's 'You Don't Bring me Flowers' and Del Shannon's 'Runaway'. Danny often had to throw his voice above a racket in Leonie's pub. Eventually he had to have nodules removed from his vocal cords. "It happens if you're in a bar scene," Patricia said, "and you're doing that on a regular basis, which of course he was."

Patricia reminisced about one memorable afternoon in the Thistle. Donna Callnan drove a yellow GTO and picked up Patricia for a late lunch. The Thistle's parking lot was empty at one-thirty and no one was in the pub. They ordered drinks at the Dory Bar and leafed through a menu. A pal pulled in next to Donna's distinctive car and joined them at the bar. Other friends dropped by.

"Let's sing," Danny Beal said and beckoned to Patricia.

Music wafted down Oak Street. Soon the place was mobbed, even the back dining room was full. Danny was near the end of a Broadway tune when a huge broad-chested fellow came in, an opera singer in a suede vest with a fringe that twirled around. He stood by the piano and broke into 'Ol' Man River'. A reverent hush fell as his deep bass tones resonated around the room.

"It was the most amazing thing," Patricia said. "Here we are, this place is packed on a Tuesday afternoon. Nobody's at work and we're all in the Thistle listening to this man who had the most magnificent voice. But that was the magic of the Thistle. People want to connect and that was the place. There's always been these other places that opened but none of them had that magnetism and draw that the Thistle had. That's what made it unique. I spent a lot of time there when I was younger. It was the place to go."

Danny Beal had a regular Wednesday night slot at the Thistle. In summer his voice wafted through my open windows. I trotted across the road to join him. He had a huge repertoire, from upbeat top ten hits to slow melodies from musicals. Barmaid Karen Perkins inched her way through the throng around the piano to collect his tips in a jar.

Danny captured the essence of the Thistle in an interview for our local newspaper. "It was like *Cheers* before the show was ever on the air with lots of colorful characters. Leonie had a wonderful old piano. I can still remember my first song there. I looked around the room and sang, 'Behind Closed Doors' [by Charlie Rich]."

Danny had a Downeast sense of humor and told anecdotes between tunes. Elton John's 'Rocket Man' was the Bigelow Lab's song. Danny winked at us when he sang the verse, 'And all this science I don't understand, it's just my job five days a week.' Danny had a gimmick. He made a call on the rotary wall phone behind the bar and never touched the dial. He tapped the numbers on a hook switch to connect. He learned that from Bobby Rice. Danny shared a rental with two pals above Wheeler's Drug Store, a two-minute stroll from the Thistle. He had a following. A gang of them rolled down the hill after Danny's last set up to his apartment. More than a dozen lads sometimes slept in his living room.

Others played piano at the Thistle. Joe Bardeau was self-taught and learned melodies by ear. He made doughnuts at the Ebbtide Restaurant each morning and was at the Thistle in the evening. Joe, fondly known as Doughnut Man, belted out sixties and seventies tunes. Customers rewarded him with drinks. On the side, Joe filled in as cook when Chef Brock vacationed in Florida. Bob Page played a mean stride piano at the Thistle. One time he was accompanied by Bigelow's Barney Balch on trombone.

George Bourette gleaned a few tips from Leonie when he opened the Carriage House, a pub and restaurant in East Boothbay. George gave Leonie credit that she never switched to soda guns and always had superior brands of bottled mixers.

Maine's DUI laws were less severe in the seventies. Servers at the Dory Bar never used a shot glass or pour spout, turbo-charged cocktails were measured by hand. Bruce Tindal recalled his usual drink, a bourbon and water, came up to a rim of his glass and was almost all booze. "It's no wonder Leonie never made any money. If she'd had more restraint, instead of selling two drinks she could have sold three or four."

Roadies, drinks to go, were popular at the Thistle. One couple told Bobby Rice they were off to Québec city. "So that's five hours right?" Bobby said and poured a slug of booze for each town along the way.

A fisherman marveled that there weren't more accidents in that era. "It's almost a statement of innocence. We probably weren't drivin' fast enough."

As a result the Dory Bar often ran out of glasses and some of Leonie's ads included an offer; if you brought one back your first drink was on the house. Her cover fee for special entertainment was a Thistle glass or one dollar.

My first Maine winter was cold enough to freeze the marrow in my bones. My decision to live in America nagged at me; I always spent Christmas with my family. But as I stood knee-deep in snow on my back porch, I realized I was home. Friendships had been made at the Thistle, not just with the Bigelow gang, but with locals too and people who had moved into town like me. I could hardly wait to buy my first real Christmas tree. They cost a fortune in Liverpool and Dad only had a bottle-brush table-top one from Woolworth's. I was as giddy as a kid, my Maine spruce was twice as tall as me. I threw a party. Pals arrived armed with drinks from the Thistle.

Leonie handed me a cardboard box for 'borrowed glasses' and refused to serve me until I brought them back.

Leonie was a vocal contributor at town meetings at the Opera House, a five-minute walk from the Thistle. Her customers went there for the verbal fireworks. "Leonie got into shouting matches," one of them recalled. "It was more entertaining than television."

A battle broke out when McSeagulls waterfront restaurant applied for a liquor license. Leonie led the charge. Her business would take a hit if they succeeded. Boothbay Harbor's Board of Selectmen denied McSeagull's request. The case went to Superior Court. They received their permit in 1977 and became the Thistle Inn's major competitor.

Maine's drinking age reverted to twenty-one in 1977 and Leonie became a selectman for Boothbay Harbor. Only the second woman to hold the office. Bobby Rice baited Leonie with, "Well I heard the town was . . ." and off she went.

Leonie used newspaper notices to encourage Boothbay Harbor residents to become more involved in town affairs. "More people should attend hearings and meetings," she said. "It could be an illuminating experience . . . and a chance to get out your boxing gloves.

"Don't tell me that there are no people with the time and brains to contribute towards our future. There are a couple of days left to put your papers in for two open selectmen positions . . . please, please do so. Caring – that's what it's all about."

She also admitted, "One of the most difficult things I have had to adjust since being elected selectman is diplomacy . . . or to be blunt, keeping my mouth shut."

Robbie Burns, a cat, moved into Leonie's Southport Island cottage. She also bought Loren, a stuffed hippopotamus, from Boothbay's Fall Foliage Festival and sat her down behind the bar. "Loren has already ingratiated herself with customers," Leonie reported in the newspaper. "She always listens, never talks and is perpetually happy."

Then Leonie bought a pig. She named her Blossom, her own nickname as a kid. The pig was intended as a gift for one of her crew, but turns out his wife already had her hands full with a new baby and Blossom was returned to the inn.

"I've no idea what was in Leonie's mind," said Bobby Rice. "But someone told her that pigs were smart. And I mentioned how idiotic it was that some university guys got a government grant to study what pigs liked to drink best. Apparently they liked screwdrivers and it took all our tax dollars to find that out." (Hogs were used in alcoholism trials at the University of Missouri and some developed a quart-a-day habit.)

"We want all of you to come and meet Blossom, our pig," Leonie said in the *Boothbay Register*. "Tremendous personality and I think will keep us from being bored this winter."

Leonie walked Blossom on a leash down Oak Street or carried her pig around the pub on its back like a baby. Blossom hated that. "She'll stop squealing if you turn her backside up," Chris Garside told Leonie in a harsh tone. The incessant noise had made him lose a hand of bridge.

The pig sat next to Leonie in the pub. If anyone complained Leonie told them, "She's a lot cleaner than most people."

"You have a pig in here," Bobby said. "Dogs aren't allowed and you've got a pig runnin' round." If Blossom made a mess on the floor, Bobby insisted that Leonie clean it up.

Leonie took Blossom to Monhegan Island on the *Balmy Days* ferry. Pigs were bad luck on a boat but no one said anything. Nobody wanted to mess with Leonie. Blossom gobbled up kitchen scraps. Her girth expanded. Leonie had a pen built just off the Harness Room and kept the door back there open for customers to admire the pig. Diners complained the pungent smell had put them off their meal and townspeople also objected to a hairy hog on the premises. Maine's Department of Health issued an ultimatum to get rid of the pig.

A lobsterman on Monhegan Island offered to take Blossom out there. Animals ran free on Manana Island, a grassy hump off Monhegan. Leonie fretted over the pig's departure, but was relieved by reports that Blossom enjoyed boat trips to the main island, was completely house-trained and had learned to climb a ladder. She also found a handsome pig husband and had twelve pig kids. Leonie advertised a costume party, this time with a pig theme. Leonie expected Blossom or at least one of her brood to attend. Her hopes were dashed, though she was a hit as Miss Piggy and Rocky entertained everyone on the piano.

Blossom's foster parent invited Leonie to dinner on the island. Her meal was set before her, Leonie turned as white as flour.

Blossom *was* dinner.

Celebrities, such as broadcast journalist, Walter Cronkite, dropped in the Thistle. Cronkite was reported to be 'the most trusted man in America'. David Soul, a blond detective in the TV series *Starsky and Hutch,* stayed at the Thistle on his honeymoon. Jimmy Dean—the country music singer with a number one hit in the sixties as well as being an actor, TV host and sausage tycoon—vacationed in Boothbay Harbor for decades and bought rounds of drinks for the Dory Bar.

Tommy Heinsohn, who played and coached for the Boston Celtics, often came in the Thistle. "He sat at the bar," Bruce Crosby said. "Most people recognized him in the dart crowd there, but nobody went up."

And then a famous pop singer came in. "I'm playing and the place was packed," pianist Kay Brown said. "And this guy peeked around the corner of the door. He was having dinner in the Harness Room and I thought, isn't that nice, you know. So he came over finally and kept asking for requests. I spent the entire evening with him without knowing who he was. 'Don't tell her,' Bobby Rice said. 'She'll get freaked out.' And after he left Bobby said, 'D'you know who you've spent the evening with? D'you know who he is, Kay? *Art Garfunkel!*' "

Dave Phinney added, "So I was at the bar and saw a couple sitting in the booth up at the front window, a guy with a New York Yankees hat on. He got up to go to the men's room and I also had to go. So of course there was a line and we were standing together.

"So I look at him and say, 'You are who I think you are right?'

"And he goes, 'Yeah, please don't say anything.'

"And I say, 'No, no, no.'

"So he goes into the men's room first and when he comes out he says, 'So are you from around here?'

"And I say, 'We live round here.' "

Paul Simon, Art Garfunkel's singing partner no less, invited Dave to join him. He was there with Carrie Fisher, the Princess Leia of *Star Wars* and they had a room at the Thistle. They bought Dave a couple of drinks and grilled him about things to do and places to see in Boothbay Harbor. Dave sat with them for an hour or more.

"Omigod!" Dave said after they left, "I talked to Princess Leia."

Artists came to the Thistle Inn. William Kienbusch, a New York painter, stayed there for three months before he taught a semester at the University of Maine. Jamie Wyeth lived on Monhegan Island and went for a brew at the Thistle whenever he was in town. He was the third generation of acclaimed Wyeth painters to draw inspiration from the island crowned by Cathedral Woods and towering cliffs on one side. Jamie stayed at the Thistle Inn for the first Shrimp Festival in 1974. "He came in with all of us because we were in the Tug of War," Rusty Court said. "He wasn't on the team, he just came in from the island because we were all partying at the Thistle." A local girl at the Dory Bar asked Jamie for an autograph. He drew a little pig on a napkin, signed it.

Rusty's father, Lee Winslow Court, was a well-known Monhegan artist. He had a painting in Leonie's pub. Tourists stopped to admire it. "What's that?" said the wife to her husband as they stood in front of the seascape.

"It's what you call a buoy. If it's straight up it means there's a lobster in the trap and if it's leaning over its empty." Some local joker had spun her husband that line.

Artist Fritz Rockwell lived in town and was a regular at the Thistle. He wore a black eyepatch that made him look like a buccaneer. Rumors were a jealous husband had shot out his eye. Nonetheless his paintings had bold form and color. When he was broke, he peddled them at the Thistle. He was also a fine sculptor. His stone lions defend steps in a driveway off Route 96, opposite the Mill Pond in East Boothbay. "Fritz spent a lot of time at the Thistle," musician Kay Brown said. "He felt at home, but he liked to have me play his favorite song, 'Tennessee Waltz,' and he'd get up and dance by himself around the bar. My God, he was so funny. That was his thing."

Artist Herb Maynard virtually lived at the inn. Leonie was fond of Herb even though he often acted out. He bartered seascapes for drinks and one of his watercolors hung in the pub. Herb requested 'Misty,' when Kay Brown played piano. He was a fan of W. B. Yeats and could recite his poems. 'The Lake Isle of Innisfree' was one of his favorites. Dave Phinney, a scientist at Bigelow Lab, recalled a fascinating conversation with Herb Maynard at the Dory Bar. He had all these interesting names for paint colors, while Dave studied how various types of marine floating plants (phytoplankton) absorb different wavelengths of light. "So we're sitting there banging these things back and forth," said Dave, "like the changeover from blue to green is such an unusual color and Herb had a name for that."

"Bars have a personality just like people," oil painter Mitch Billis said. "The Thistle was a great place." His grandmother ran a speakeasy during Prohibition in a predominantly Italian town in upstate New York. Mitch was brought up in the Billis Hotel, where his dad served drinks and his mother waited tables. A swing door led to their ground floor apartment and the family ate most of their meals in the saloon. Mitch rode his tricycle throughout the taproom. When he was older he did homework at a corner booth. He became a math professor then took up art.

Mitch was one of the Thistle Inn's late night crowd. "So I was used to spending time in a bar, it felt like home to me. I got my fix after I got through painting and I'd have one beer, sometimes two and then walk home."

Mitch often paints in Europe. "I was on a plane once going to Italy, right, and I'm sitting next to somebody and the guy said, 'Where you from?'

"And I said, 'Boothbay Harbor.'

"And he said, 'Omigod, the Thistle.' "

Strohn Woodard sometimes hung out with Mitch Billis at the Dory Bar. "Because I was trying to be a novelist," Strohn said, "I worked fairly late at night, up until ten or something, and then I'd go in there for a nightcap so I'd sleep. Bobby's playing poker with Jo Pallino in the corner. And there was this guy sitting at the bar, a transvestite, makeup on, long blond hair, and in a dress that would have been passable in another context. But his hands were even shorter and more muscular than mine and he's clenching them because nobody's paying him any attention. He thought he was making a statement of some kind, and nobody cared. He left, didn't even finish his beer.

"People I had imagined in my novel were more real to me than people actually there."

On another late night scene Bobby was in a poker game at the front table as usual, when three young drunks staggered in. "You've had enough to drink," Bobby said. "No more drinks."

"To hell yer won't," they said. "We'll fight this out in the parkin' lot."

Bobby stared right at them. Then pulverized his cigarette in an ashtray like it was their faces.

"We'll see yer," they said.

Memorable characters spiced up the flavor of Leonie's inn.

Extra dry martinis were one older couple's favorite tipple. Both were well groomed and their mannerisms suggested a genteel background. They ordered cocktails while they waited for their food. Curious glances were thrown their way when the couple's expressions darkened and they leant towards each other across the table, knuckles white as they clenched their glasses.

She tipped her cocktail on her husband's head.

He threw his at her.

A waitress bustled in and the wife said, in her quiet cultured way, "We'd like another round here, please."

Then there was a lanky businessman who strode into Leonie's saloon on his lunchbreak and worked on a crossword. Some customers were impressed that he completed puzzles quickly. The word whiz left without his newspaper one day and when Bobby Rice cleared the table he found the crossword filled with gibberish.

A former stockbroker came in every lunchtime. His classic line was, "A working man deserves an occasional cocktail." One day he was there all afternoon with a pal. At five-clock they tossed back their vodkas and said, "We gotta go, we've gotta go to an AA meeting."

Bull Dodge, appropriately named, with thighs like tree trunks, was always at the Thistle. One night he lost his false teeth. Bull came in to look for them next day when the pub was empty. He searched everywhere but never found them and no one had handed them in. A week later Dean Morrison wound up on the floor. His head was under the piano. "Bull," he said, "I have good news for you. I've found your teeth."

One of Leonie's regulars had been a squadron commander in the U.S. Airforce. He lived in Boothbay Harbor when he retired and took tourists out on his sailboat. The flier had all the characteristics of a fearless top gun and often grumbled at the Dory Bar about a fellow combat pilot who had gained fame, Chuck Yeager. "*I* never got shot down," the Boothbay veteran said. "I got shot up a lot, but I never got shot down like *him*."

Then there was a wily sea captain who stood up to leave and threw a stack of bills on the counter.

"You can't drive," Bobby Rice said. "You've been here all day."

"I'm fine, I'm fine."

"You're so drunk you won't be able to start your car."

The captain winked, "I know, that's why I kept it runnin'."

Leonie had trained in business, but beneath her tough exterior she was soft as Jell-O. She often fell for a tale of woe and let regulars run up tabs. These chits were kept in a set of wooden boxes, intended for room keys, next to the till. Some were never honored.

Ian Morris, Bigelow's research director, held court at the back corner table in the pub. He bought rounds of drinks and invited people to join him for dinner. He treated everyone night after night and handed Leonie his paycheck every month to settle his tab. Leonie extended Ian's credit when he divorced. He owed a staggering amount. Food was only a tenth of his bar tab.

Bigelow seminars were held on Friday mornings. Lunch was at the Thistle. Peter Larsen had been to a science conference. He arrived back in town at eleven-thirty on Friday and went straight to the Thistle. He took the window booth in the pub and waited for the Bigelow regulars. A couple of State enforcement guys in uniform barged in, went to the back of the bar and looked at customers' tabs.

"Whose is this?" one officer asked Bobby Rice.

"Oh he's not here."

"Whose is this, is he here?"

Bobby nodded at Peter, "Uh-huh, that's him over there."

"Okay, and he had this to drink today?"

"That's right."

"Six martinis and twelve Budweiser?"

"Well, he's been here since ten o'clock."

The officer glared and shut the place down for a week. (Maine Law banned drinks on credit.)

I arranged to meet Ian Morris for a working lunch at the Thistle. The pub was almost empty when I arrived. "Where is everyone?" I asked Bobby Rice.

"It's Voting Day. You can't buy booze until the polls close."

Sunday liquor sales were also prohibited in the mid-seventies. One card player had a long face that day. He had screwed up and voted to continue the Sunday ban.

Jack Laird, a crusty ex-Navy guy, was Bigelow Lab's marine technician. He stopped for a beer in the Thistle on his way from work. Jack took scientists out each week on Bigelow's research vessel to monitor seasonal changes in coastal waters. Ian Morris called the closest sampling site to Boothbay Harbor Station Ale, for after Jack docked everyone headed to the Thistle.

Jack teased me about my odd English sayings. This began on a week-long cruise in the Gulf of Maine. I needed to take dawn samples and wanted Jack to knock on my cabin door to wake me up.

"Knock me up at five in the morning, will you?" I said to Jack.

"Sure, I'd be glad to," he said.

The next time Jack was at the Thistle, he told this anecdote to Bobby Rice. I never lived that down.

Ian joked that he could hear me before I came in a room and if I sat on my hands I would be unable to speak. I was in the middle of a story in the pub and knocked over a glass of wine.

"I think another round is in order," Ian said and stood up to go to the bar.

"You know she only does that when she first comes in," Bobby Rice said of my talking with my hands and spilling drinks. "It's not because she's drunk."

Ian drew columns on a Thistle place mat with headings: date, time, drinks consumed and number of spills.

Data were never collected.

Linda Sapienza worked for Peter Larsen at Bigelow Lab. She peered down a microscope for hours on end to examine diversity in populations of tiny animals that lived in marine sediments. Her job was tedious. Sometimes she persuaded Peter to have lunch at the Thistle where she hoped to stay all afternoon. "It sometimes happened," she said. "The Thistle had that kind of pull."

Brock's burgers and steak sandwiches were a hit with Bigelow Lab's regulars. Shelley Orne, our usual lunchtime waitress, balanced several plates like an octopus.

"She's very efficient," Ian Morris said. "She'd make a great lab-tech."

Shelley's tongue was as sharp as a carving knife. If you asked about specials she said, "But yer don't want that," and offered her own suggestion. Her deadpan expression cracked when she smiled and she had a dry sense of humor. She expected a reasonable reward for her service and if someone tried to stiff her she said, "Tipping is not a city in China."

Brock came back from vacation in the southwest and spiced up the Thistle's menu with a few Mexican specials. He played cards in the pub on a slow night. A waitress interrupted him only if she had an order. "Yeah-yeah-yeah," he said and carried on until he finished his hand. Brock had his priorities.

I dreamed about Brock's food when I was out for a month at sea, especially on Duke University's vessel, the *Eastward*. When you work sixteen-hour days with no weekends off, food is one of your few pleasures. Meals at the Thistle were to die for and meals on the *Eastward* could kill you. They swam in grease and the only veggies were grits and canned black-eyed peas. We hoofed it to the Thistle as soon as we docked at Wotton's Wharf in Boothbay Harbor. I could already taste

Brock's scallops, flambéed in brandy with mounds of fresh vegetables, before I opened the front door.

Most of Bigelow Lab's scientists were from out of state and when their parents came to visit they took them for a meal at the Thistle.

Carmen Sapienza was a grad student in a work-study program with the University of Maine. His parents came from Pittsburgh, where restaurants competed for the biggest, baddest, fish sandwich.

"Okay this fish sandwich is it a generous portion of fish or bite-sized pieces that they cut out?" Carmen's dad said to Shelley.

"Dad, its real pieces of fish."

"Are you sure?" his dad said.

Shelley glared and refused to comment, slammed down a plate loaded with haddock in front of him and stalked off.

Peter Larsen recalled the first time he took his folks to Leonie's inn. "My parents had just moved up here and they got here kind of late, it was dark. And I said, 'Let's go down to the Thistle and get something to eat.' So we go in and the place is packed, 'cause it's Shrimp Festival. And I thought this is hopeless but they made room for us at the lab table, in the corner there. The kitchen was about to close, but they insisted that they could do food for us. I was impressed by that. It really was a home away from home."

When Jeff Brown's mother drove up from Massachusetts, he suggested a late dinner at the Thistle. Jeff had just joined Bigelow Lab and this was his first time at Leonie's pub. Weather was warm and windows were flung open. They were seated at a table near the bow of the Dory Bar when two guys began to shove and push each other. One picked up the other and tossed him out a window. Leonie stormed out to scold them, came back in and apologized to the customers.

"Do those guys know each other?" asked Jeff's mother.

"They know each other alright – they're brothers," said Leonie.

My mother came to visit, her first time in the States. I picked her up from Logan Airport in my dilapidated VW Bug bought for five hundred dollars.

"Oh Hilary, I'm so excited. It's all so different," she said as we drove along. "I've always wanted to travel, but Dad was never keen. It was very good of him to let me come on my own, you know."

"We'll have fun. I've taken a few days off work to show you round."

"Good heavens," she said when we drove by a huge statue, a Native American Indian in a feathered headdress. I pulled over and took a photo of her next to the roadside attraction in South Freeport.

My landladies had offered me a sweet deal and I had just bought the house on Oak Street across from the Thistle. Mother was impressed. She and Dad rented their home in Liverpool, England, and a cramped attic in a Victorian row house had been all I could afford to rent in London.

Mum stared at all the clapboard houses with chimneys along Oak Street. "Aren't you afraid of your house burning down?" she said as I carried her suitcase through my front door. (After the Great Fire of London, wooden dwellings were replaced by brick.) She had also nearly lost her home in the 1940 Blitz. A bomb hit an ammunition train near her street and fire broke out on her roof.

To ease her mind, I took her to the Thistle to meet my friends. "Mum, what would you like to drink?"

"I'll have an American cocktail please, I've never had one."

Mum had a sweet tooth, I chose a White Russian. Bobby Rice poured a lot of vodka for Mum, a five foot featherweight.

"I'm sorry Hilary, I have to go and lie down. That jetlag has done me in."

My father accompanied her the next time she came to visit. I took them to the Thistle, but Dad refused to buy Mum a White Russian.

"I'm not getting her that, I don't know what's in it," he said and ordered her a port and lemon.

Bobby shrugged.

"Port with lemonade," my father said by way of explanation.

"Dad, don't, it's not the same over here."

He ignored my advice. Dad liked to be in charge. Mum took a sip and grimaced. Dad had expected British fizzy lemonade – like American 7-Up.

My visiting parents raved about American ice cream. They always chose that for 'afters' at the Thistle Inn and bought cones at Porter's Drug Store every afternoon. Mum tried every flavor, Dad always had vanilla. "Best to stick with what you know," was my father's motto . . . unless it was port with lemonade!

"Yes!" I punched the air with my fist and dashed out of my office to share the news. My first grant from an American funding agency had come through. "I'll meet you guys at the Thistle, drinks are on me."

As soon as I walked in the pub I bought a round for the bar. The Yentsch's younger son arrived when we were at dinner. The tow-headed seven-year-old presented me with a bunch of brightly colored balloons. Clarice, Charlie's wife, had sent him inside while she waited outside in her car. I was grateful to her, she had paid me part-time while I applied for U.S. research funding.

Years later, a friend and I met a guy at a bar in Portsmouth, New Hampshire. "Weren't you the gal who bought drinks for everyone at the Thistle?" he said.

Rhonda Selvin was in my research group for a while. She served our Bigelow crowd at the Thistle and those conversations convinced her to take a job at the lab. "Leonie wasn't too happy about that," Rhonda said. "She liked me a lot — I'm not really sure why, but she did. Bobby was always saying, 'She thinks you're a princess, I've no idea why she likes you so much.'"

"We didn't make that many cocktails unless it was Happy Hour," Rhonda said. "At that time people mostly drank martinis. Tap beer was not available, people either had a bottle of ale or a house wine. You didn't go to the Thistle to have a rare wine, you went there to have a rare experience." Rhonda had to walk a mile to work in blizzards. The Thistle was the only place open and everyone tried to get there. "It wasn't like you got a snow day from the Thistle," she said. "And when you got there it was wonderful. The fire was going and it was so warm, there was food, everybody in the world was there. Blizzards were awesome." Snow storms never fazed me, my house was close to the Thistle. Others cross-country skied to get there if roads were bad.

The bartenders, led by Bobby and Leonie, paid close attention to how much people drank, Rhonda said. They cared. "We shut a lot of people off and they just stayed and hung around 'cause it was the friendliest place in the world to be." Rhonda ensured customers had a ride home, if needed. "There was a wonderful camaraderie, people looked out for each other." Nobody gave Rhonda a hard time. Patrons had enormous respect for the Thistle and the people who served them.

Arms crossed, Leonie's emotions tossed about like driftwood. Rhonda had chosen the Tugboat Inn for her wedding buffet instead of the Thistle. On the morning of Rhonda's big day, Leonie flounced into her competitor's venue and pointed at their tablecloths. "These won't do," she said, as though she was mother of the bride.

The reception was a huge success despite Leonie's misgivings. She jitterbugged on a dancefloor in a velvet green jacket and a twirling plaid skirt. Strohn Woodard was one of her dance partners. "Get into it, Woodard," she said.

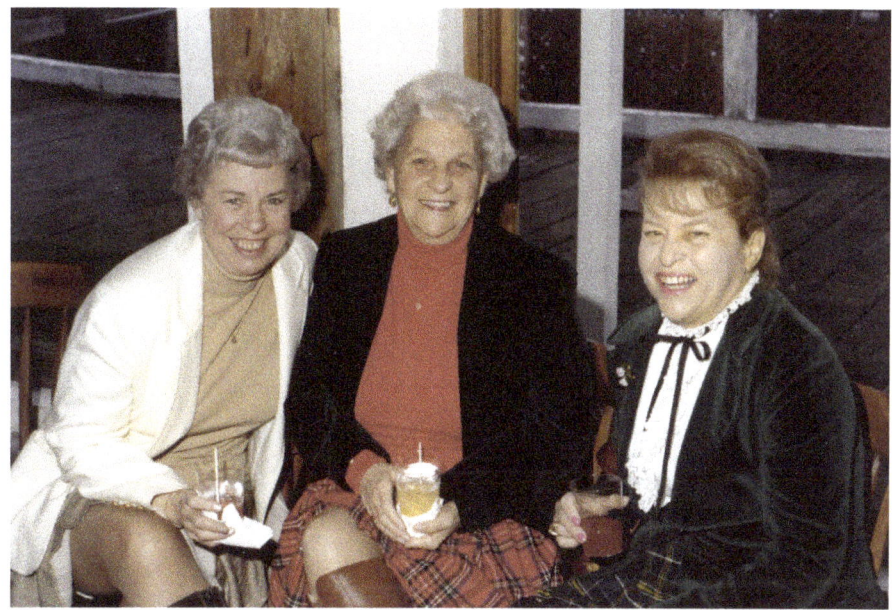

Leonie (right) and two of her waitstaff, Millie (center) and Eleanor (left) at Rhonda's wedding reception. 1980. (Courtesy of Rhonda Selvin)

"I first got interested in the Thistle," said George Bourette, "because this was way before politically correct. There was no such thing. It was more of a therapy session when you went in there. If you did somethin' somebody brought it right out in the bar. It was public discussion and everybody was up for grabs. I loved that."

A guy might say something fresh to a gal in the pub, but in general social boundaries were respected. Except for one unforgettable occasion.

Someone grabbed my butt in the Thistle.

I spun around. My hand connected with a cheek. My eyes met a frozen expression. I had hit the wrong guy. Roars of laughter erupted. "I'm *so* sorry," I said to the shaken fellow.

I gazed along the barstools at Douglas Carter, his hands the size of dinner plates.

"It wasn't me," he said.

Rounds were bought at the Dory Bar when fishermen hauled an enormous catch or hunters bagged a deer. Tradesmen were difficult to pin down during hunting season. Pierce and Hartung, a hardware and lumber company, advertised sports equipment in November's *Region Aires*.

Chris Garside bought a shotgun and took vacation days from Bigelow Lab. His female technician glowered and called him The Dark-side, a Bambi killer. The Garsides were from England and had never cooked a turkey in the U.S. Chris picked one up for Thanksgiving from the market. "Where's the loose giblets for the gravy?" he said to his wife, Jean, when he unwrapped the bird at home. He jumped in his car and headed back to town to buy some chicken livers. Unsuccessful, he stopped for a couple of beers at the Thistle. He hit Bambi with his car on his way home, along route 238 on Southport Island. The radiator was completely smashed. His lab tech thought that was poetic justice.

The following day Chris unknowingly cooked a plastic packet of giblets in the turkey. The Thistle went wild about that story and never let him forget.

Logs blazed in cast-iron stoves on winter holidays at the Thistle. Bigelow Lab held the annual Christmas party there. Leonie also put on a feast for lab people who were in between relationships or had no family in town. "She had a good heart," Peter Larsen said. "And knew we'd be alone and opened her doors for us."

One Christmas Leonie invited Bigelow's Brits to a private celebration. Her first husband, an English actor and London radio director, had come to visit and she wanted us to meet him. Leonie's second ex was also there, a charismatic Italian who came up from New York each year to help Leonie with her taxes. Husband number one, in a velvet smoking jacket and silk cravat, entertained us with humorous anecdotes after dinner. Leonie played a vinyl LP of Dylan Thomas's *A Child's Christmas in Wales*. The lyrical timbre of Dylan's voice was powerful. Ian Morris's eyes grew moist at his own boyhood memories in a Welsh coalminer's cottage.

Christmas lights winked behind the Dory Bar. "A white wine, please," I said to barmaid Karen Perkins. "And a round for that lot." I nodded towards Bigelow Lab's table.

I sat down next to Jean Garside, an English math whiz. "So what's new?" Jean said to me.

"I'm going to have a stab at sugar mice for my tree. I'll use salt dough though, so they'll keep for next year."

Susan Sykes frowned. "What are you making?"

"Cute candy mice," Jean said. "They're English stocking stuffers and come in pastel shades."

My objective, to have only one drink, had fallen flat well before Ian Morris ordered another round. "Not for me," I said, "I've gotta go."

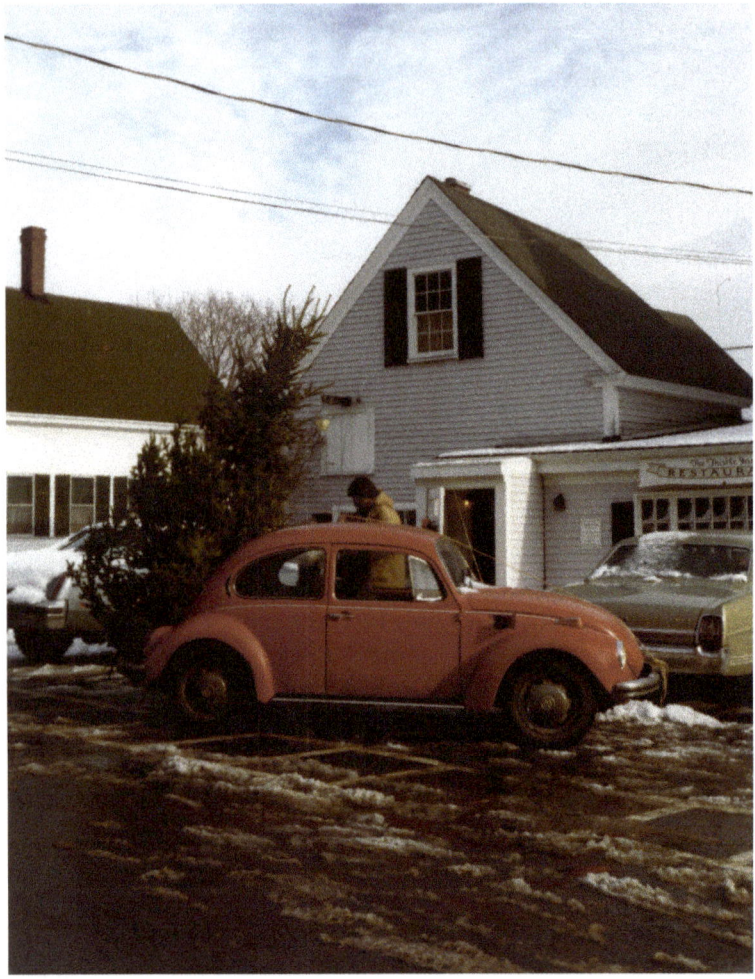

Christmas tree on my VW Bug in the Thistle's parking lot. Mark Cole (by my car). 1979. Hilary E. Bartlett.

Back home I made dough and molded mice, currants for eyes and white string for tails. I came in the kitchen next morning. They were large and had great haunches, were overcooked and a yucky shade of brown.

Rats! Foiled by the lure of the Thistle.

New Year's Eve at Leonie's inn was a roast beef buffet, champagne and revelers in silly hats with paper blowouts. Some years they had live music. Customers danced to upbeat hits, with a slow waltz or two thrown in for a change of pace. Leonie stood on top of the Dory Bar for the ritual countdown. She released balloons at midnight to cheers, toots and blares, hugs and kisses. Magnums of bubbly were opened. Many patrons booked a room.

On St. Paddy's Day Danny Beal played Irish ditties. Glasses of Irish coffee were served and foaming pitchers of green beer, once Leonie had draft ale on tap. Corned beef with cabbage was the special. I shuddered. English corned beef came in cans, a gelatinized mass of cheap meat. My aunties had served that in the fifties, when larders were full of tins left over from the war. I had a lot to learn about America; cured brisket was one of them. Most of Leonie's customers wore emerald green. She and her beagles dressed in orange, either to support Ireland's Protestant minority or Leonie liked to be different.

April Fools' Day parties were held in the Dory Bar unless that date conflicted with Fishermen's Festival. ". . . we can always celebrate being fools any-time," Leonie said when she canceled.

A special dinner was prepared for Easter, glazed ham with raisin sauce or tender roast lamb, for die-hard beef lovers a Robbie Burns steak. Some years they had a Mother's Day Special.

"Have a wonderful July 4th weekend," Leonie wrote in a newspaper ad. "And don't forget to drop in and wet your whistle, but the restaurant will not be serving meals." She gave her staff the day off. All except Bobby Rice who had to tend bar.

Leonie's Halloween costumes were haunting. Once she wore a pointed black hat, dangly spider earrings, a short black dress and fishnet tights, more flirtatious than the real Oz's Wicked Witch of the West, the actress Margaret Hamilton who lived on Cape Island off the tip of Southport.

Leonie jumped up on the Dory Bar at midnight and said, "Free champagne for everybody."

Bobby Rice tugged her skirt, "Leonie, we don't have any — we've run out."

Another year she held a *Star Wars* theme party after the cocktail lounge scene. Getups were so outrageous that *everyone* received a gift certificate instead of only one or two.

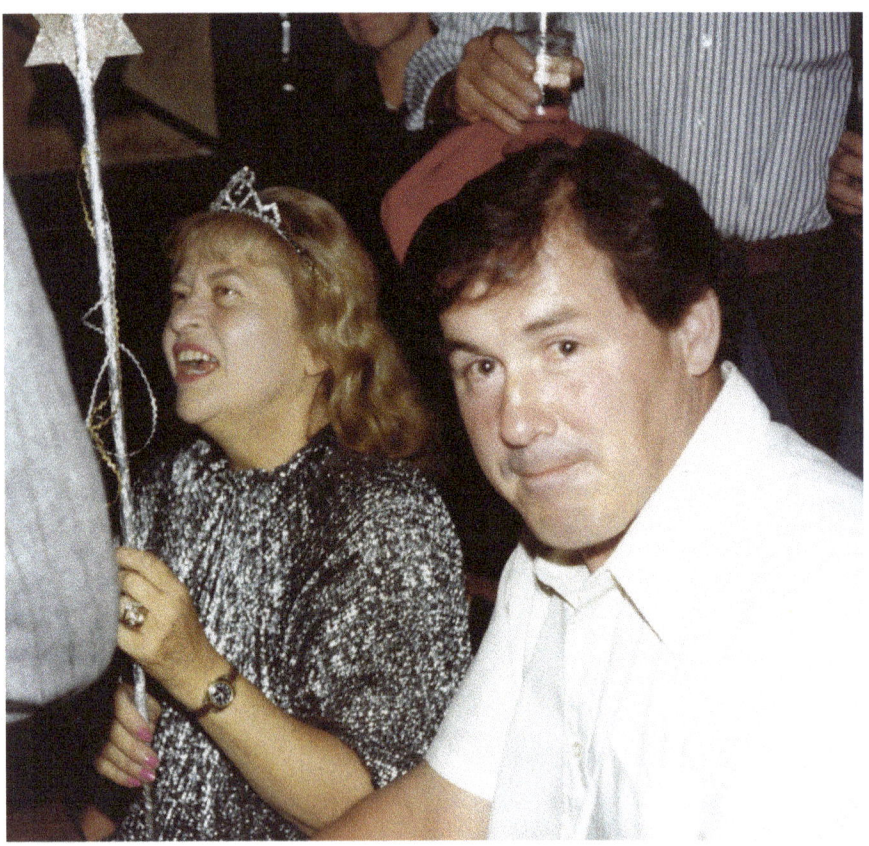

Leonie at her birthday party with head bartender, Bobby Rice. 1981. Hilary E. Bartlett.

Leonie always made a big splash on her birthday. One year she wore a silver lamé dress with a sparkling tiara wedged on her curls. We drank bubbly and Brock made a cake with dark chocolate frosting — the closest thing to Leonie's request for a black topping.

Danny Beal broke into Stevie Wonder's 'Happy Birthday' when I walked in the Thistle at Happy Hour. Rocky, piano player and mailman, approached with a shit-eating grin. "You've gotta gift from England," he said and handed me a parcel addressed in Mother's handwriting. She had clued Rocky in with a detailed description on the Customs' label. I tore at the brown paper wrapping. Hoots and hollas erupted as a naughty piece of lingerie fell out, my face as red as the low-cut slippery teddy clasped in my hands.

"Your *mother* sent you *that*!" said Lee Doggett as she looked down at her preppie skirt and wool knee socks stuffed into penny loafers.

Other jaws had dropped around our table. All my friends had met my mother in the Thistle. A demure, conservative, English lady who tried to eat a hamburger with a knife and fork.

Bobby won the Tall Tales contest and the Bartenders Golf Tournament in 1978. After that Leonie referred to him as King. Mike Jarrett, at the Dory Bar, bragged he was the toughest guy in Boothbay Harbor. Bobby came out from behind the counter and knocked him down. Mike stood up, shook his head and said, "Well . . . I'm the second toughest guy in town."

Money troubles kept Leonie awake at nights. Spats with Bobby often started when she was worried about the inn's finances. One afternoon she stormed in the pub with an avalanche of complaints. Bobby's eyes turned as black as coal. He taunted her with no mercy until she cried. "*Nobody* interrupts my cribbage game," Bobby said.

She stomped upstairs.

But Bobby and Leonie depended on each other. Once he tried to stop her driving after she had been drinking. Leonie ignored him and jumped in her Lincoln. Bobby picked up the phone.

"Did you know Bobby turned me in to the cops?" Leonie said to Linda Sapienza a few days later. "Told them the Continental was on the move." She glared at Bobby behind the bar. Her lower lip quivered, "Then, when I called him from jail he left me there *all night.* I'm not talking to Bobby."

He had turned her in and refused to bail her out.

One night I heard a crunch outside my house; footsteps on packed snow. I shivered and dialed 999, (the U.K. emergency number). "Why can't I get through?" I forgot it was 911.

After I convinced myself the creep had left, I bolted to the Thistle and told Bobby Rice. He wrote down the inn's phone number for me. "Go back an' stick this on your phone," he said. "Then I'll serve you." Bobby knew the Thistle guys could get to my place on the hill across the street faster than the cops. I kept the Thistle's number on my phone until I moved a few miles away in 1982.

All of Leonie's regulars knew the Thistle's phone number, 3541. Boothbay's numbers began with 633 but that did not need to be dialed. Thistle patrons also called from out of state.

"Hilary, it's Jack Chagan," Bobby said and handed me the receiver.

"Hi, I thought you were in Florida."

"I am. I need your recipe for duck with orange sauce."

Servers passed on phone messages or covered for a customer. "He's on his way," was the usual line for every bar widow on the other end.

"I never cared for the place," one wife said. "I was tendin' our kids at home an' my husband was down at the Thistle."

Leonie's mother died. She was eighty-six. Leonie kept the ashes in an urn on a bookshelf in her living room opposite room one on the ground floor. Mrs. Adams had given her daughter a book when she graduated high school. An inscription said, "To Thy Own Self Be True." Leonie lived up to that. To hell with what people might say.

Leonie was in the pub one Saturday with two women friends. They compared warm March temperatures in Florida with a chilly mud season in Maine. Inspiration struck when Leonie walked out of the Thistle arm in arm with her girlfriends and left their menfolk inside. Later that night the guys received a long distance phone call at the Dory Bar. Their ladies were in Miami. Leonie's inducement had been too enticing to ignore. Forget the husbands, Leonie wanted to party with her gal pals in Florida.

Back in town Leonie rented room one to Marie Callnan to start a dress boutique, The Foxy Lady. Leonie's only reservation was she and her female crew would soon be broke with a dress shop on the premises.

Leonie advanced with an old photo album tucked under one arm. "Did I ever show you this?" she said and joined me at a booth.

"No, what is it?"

She slowly turned each page, eyes glazed lost in thought. It was a collection of black and white figure studies taken when she was young, like Alfred Stieglitz's intimate photographs of Georgia O'Keeffe.

"Leonie, you were stunning."

A former employee also told me there was a provocative photo of Leonie next to her bedroom, from when she was a showgirl at an Off Broadway club.

Leonie's dog, Angus, never left her side after Bonnie Beagle died. Angus's favorite spot was in the window booth of the pub. His party trick was to lap up beer from a cocktail glass. He also developed a taste for cigarette butts left in ashtrays.

After Mike Jarrett's dog, Skylar, died, Leonie bought him a puppy but Mike turned down her offer. The replacement, a sad-eyed basset hound, was no match for Skyler. The Garsides adopted the pup and he tagged along when we skied on the Country Club's trails.

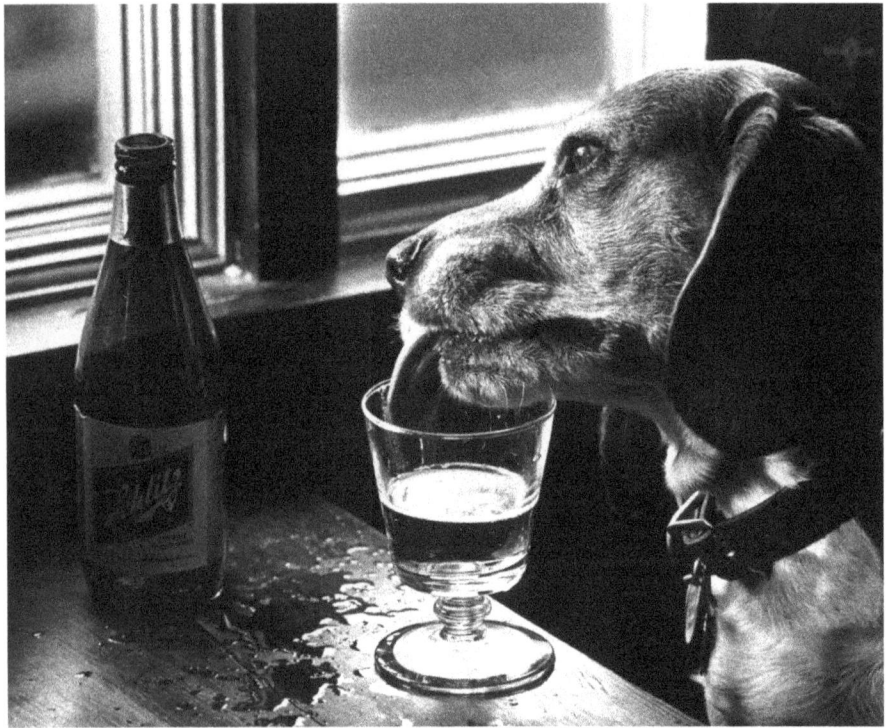

Leonie's beagle, Angus, in the pub. 1970s. Stephen Rubicam.

One of the Thistle's regulars was a dog breeder, a tall fellow with a comb-over. Passionate about hunting, he kept retrievers and hounds in kennels outside town on Boothbay's Back River.

"D'you still breed wolfdogs?" Dana Moses asked him one night in the pub.

"Sure," he said. He returned from his truck with a squirmy pup in his arms.

"He's adorable," Dana said and tickled the puppy's belly. Other women gathered round.

A couple of old salts were at the Dory Bar. "Don't sound right to me, messin' with nature," one said.

His shipmate shook his head, "Nope! A seven-eighth wolf is bound to cause a hassle."

The dog breeder split up with his wife and kept one full-grown wolfdog at his new place in East Boothbay. Trouble broke out and rumors set the Thistle alight. Some patrons claimed the animal was chained in a yard all day and howled non-stop. Nearby residents called the police. Others at the Dory Bar said the creature escaped, scared some kids and a cop had threatened to shoot it. The estranged wife saved the day. The canine was unharmed and neighbors were placated.

Her ex arrived back in town at six. She gave him hell.

My boyfriend moved in. We had a tremendous argument one Saturday afternoon and I threw him out of my house. Bandit, my dog, assumed from raised voices he had done something wrong. He ran out of an open door and bolted down the hill to the Thistle. Lee Doggett rescued him in the parking lot and stood open-mouthed as stray items sailed out over my porch railing. A suitcase burst open mid-air and shirts, pants and underclothes scattered over the hillside. Lee went back in the pub, hid Bandit under a table and reported back to her pals. Twilight settled in and the jilted lover gave up the search for his belongings. Bandit sprang up and licked my hand when I came in the Thistle. I hugged him and put him in my VW, parked unlocked at MacAndrews Gulf Station. The interior of my car was already demolished. Bandit was addicted to horse hair, had shredded it from seatbacks. I returned to the Thistle and went up to the bar. "Damn!" I had locked my front door and left my bag in the house: no money, no keys. Bobby Rice grinned at my sob story and set up a tab.

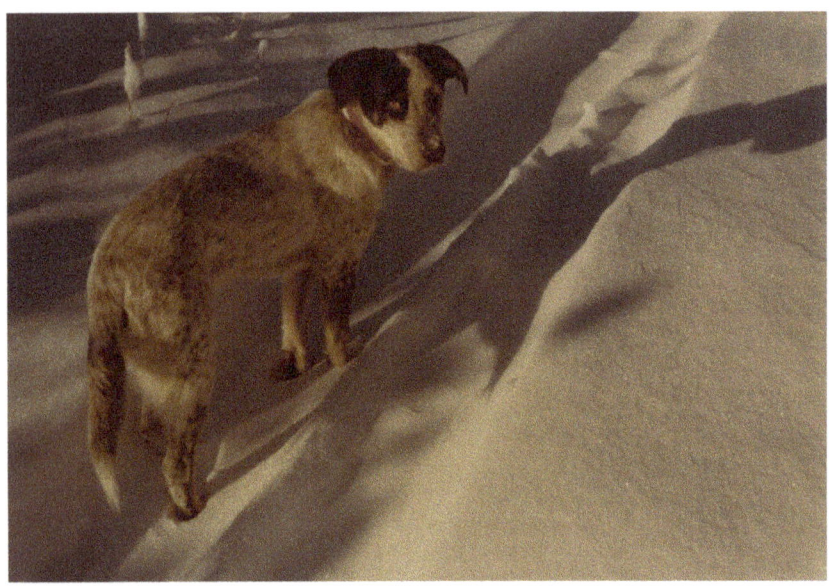

My dog, Bandit. 1980. Hilary E. Bartlett.

"You can stay the night with us," Jean Garside said. She and her husband, Chris, lived on the end of Southport Island. "Bandit too. He loves our retrievers."

Snow fell that night. We returned to town next morning, as soon as the Garside's driveway was plowed. "Thanks Chris," I said when he pulled up on Oak Street. "I owe you."

Cut to late March. A thaw arrived and we went to Happy Hour at the Thistle to celebrate the end of cabin fever. My plumber came up to our table, "Hilary, what gives? There's stuff all over yer front yard."

Blue and yellow patches peeked through melted snow on the hillside across the street.

Shirts had bloomed like spring flowers.

Leonie was often woken up by the sound of breaking glass.

Sometimes she was bighearted about a broken pane.

Other times she ranted and raved.

Sometimes she was chatty and friendly.

Other times she stormed into the pub in her nightgown before last call and yelled, "Get goddamn out of here! Why don't you go home? Don't you have a home anywhere?"

Sometimes she bought a round for everyone, another time she shut customers off at eight. She jumped up on the Dory Bar and screamed, "I want all of you out, everybody out." People chugged down drinks while Leonie hopped off the bar top and stood at the front door to herd everyone out.

Somebody broke a pane in the casement window of the pub one night. "How did that happen?" Leonie said when she came in next day. Jo Pallino, engrossed in a card game at the front table, ignored Leonie's plea for help. She commandeered Bobby Rice from behind the bar. He measured the window a little bit off. Leonie returned from Grover's Hardware, but the glass was too large. "Measure it again," she said to Bobby. This went on time after time, wrong again, wrong again. Mouth set in a hard line she paced about, arms swinging.

Bobby often teased Leonie. She always parked her car in the Thistle's parking lot and left her key in the ignition. To teach her a lesson, Bobby drove off in her Lincoln one day. When she came out of her office her vehicle was gone. "Leonie, don't you remember where your car is?" Bobby said.

"Yes, I parked it right there." She pointed to the empty space in the lot.

"Obviously you don't remember." He kept her Lincoln for three days, then drove it back to her usual spot outside the pub, left the key inside.

When she came downstairs she gasped. "My car's here."

"Of course it's here," Bobby said, "what's the matter with you?"

Old jokes went round the Thistle for recycling. Bigelow Lab's underground rag caused gales of laughter at the pub. No one escaped wisecracks from our Editor-in-Chief or his wife, Editor-in-Toxicated. Bigelow Lab was never just bricks and mortar or scientific publications. We were a family and the Thistle Inn was home.

A swing bridge connected Southport Island to the mainland. Chris Garside came up with an idea for a soap opera, *As the Bridge Turns*. "All we need is twenty-four-hour cameras at the Southport Bridge and the Thistle," he said. "With some creative editing we'd easily have enough film footage for a daily fifty-minute show."

"We'd also find out whose sneaking across the bridge at five in the morning," Lee Doggett said.

A waitress dangled a huge spider crab above the toilet in the ladies' room. Fisherman Douglas Carter upped that with a snapping turtle in the lavatory bowl. Determined to escape, the reptile pushed up the lid. Douglas chuckled. It reminded him of Oscar in *Sesame Street* with a trash can cover on his head. Douglas went to the bar, ordered a drink.

Two grey-haired waitresses screamed and dashed down the steps into the pub. Leonie followed them and confronted Douglas.

"How d'yer know it was me?" he said.

"Who else could it be?" Leonie scowled.

Despite his antics Leonie had a soft spot for Douglas. He even lent one of his dories for a Windjammer Day Parade that she was organizing.

A lad from Grey's Homestead led a dray horse along Oak Street. Douglas popped out of the pub to investigate. Since the front doors were propped open, Douglas slapped the gelding's rump and the animal bolted through the front dining room into the back one. The old floorboards groaned under the weight. Afraid the horse might fall through, Douglas snatched up the reins and backed the creature out.

Leonie became hitched a fifth time to a fellow named Jenkins, who sold chains for skidders and other logging equipment. All her regulars were invited to the wedding on Easter Sunday at the First United Methodist Church, just down the hill from the Thistle.

"Only Leonie could try to upstage Christ," a former altar boy said with a grin.

Danny Beal played 'Desperado' on the organ as she walked down the aisle in a long, ivory, lace gown with dyed shoes to match. Afterward, at a boisterous reception with an open bar up at the Thistle, Danny said, "I've always wanted to do that."

Guests spilled into the parking lot. Scores of empty champagne bottles piled up in Mike Jarrett's convertible. Everyone went back in for the cake cutting ceremony. Leonie spoofed that up. She had so much fun at her party that she almost missed her honeymoon.

Linda and Carmen Sapienza, formerly of Bigelow Lab, had a significant bar tab at the Thistle when they left Maine. Leonie never asked them to pay up but Linda mailed her three separate checks to settle their bill. Whenever the Sapienzas came back to Boothbay Harbor, they went to the Thistle to catch up on local news.

"Welcome back," Bobby Rice said and filled them in on Blossom's demise while he fixed their drinks.

Leonie sat down next to Linda under the Cuckolds life ring. "I've got something to show you," she said and opened an ivory album edged in gold.

Bobby Rice interrupted, "Oh yeah, she got married again too."

"Congratulations," Linda said.

Bobby shook his head and cleaned a glass. Leonie gave Linda a blow-by-blow account as she leafed through the album.

"And who's this?" Linda said and pointed at an attractive woman who held the groom's hand.

"My husband's mother," Leonie said and quickly flipped the page. "And here, at the reception, the cake was chocolate. I thought that would be different . . ."

Bobby cut in, "Tell the part where your new husband left you."

The pub quieted, all eyes swiveled to Leonie.

She patted her French twist hairdo with lacquered pink nails. "Well he's away right now on business with his mother," she said and closed the album. "But it's okay," she said softly. "He'll be back . . . he left our son here." Her gaze fell on a sullen teenager in the corner engrossed in a video game on a huge console. This was the first time she allowed such a game in the pub. With no children of her own, Leonie spoiled him.

A week later he skedaddled. He robbed her money on the way out. But nothing held Leonie down for long. She bounced back.

Leonie walked off with a beautiful ring from her first marriage, a Greenwich Village apartment from her second, the Thistle Inn from her third and a waterfront home from her fourth. Her luck ran out on the fifth.

Leonie never divorced Jenkins. She remained separated to prevent herself marrying a sixth time. "She never got over T'Donald," Bobby Rice said. "It was all downhill after that."

For years Charlie Yentsch, Bigelow Lab's founder, had scrawled graphs on the back (white side) of Leonie's red paper placemats. He always asked for more and went through dozens. We were just as bad. Then one day she presented us with these new black and white placemats made up as graph paper. Written near the bottom (in a bold font) the Thistle Inn was stated to be an institute for ocean sciences and Leonie had put bogus letters for academic degrees and awards after her name. From then on, servers always gave us these special placemats.

Charlie acknowledged this in Proceedings of the 1980 Brookhaven Symposium in New York, *Primary Productivity in the Sea*. "Many of the ideas set forth here came from discussions with my colleagues at Bigelow, generally at the Thistle Inn during lunch where the proprietress, Dame Leonie Greenwood-Adams Jenkins, irritated by the constant doodling on the table tops and napkins, now has placemats made up as graph paper."

We used them to work out ideas. One session in the pub led me to work on a project with Chris Garside. Bets were made on how long we would last, we often clashed. But we got funded and beat the odds; our partnership lasted two years. Many collaborations were forged at the Thistle Inn, some with visiting scientists. All led to publications in textbooks or journals.

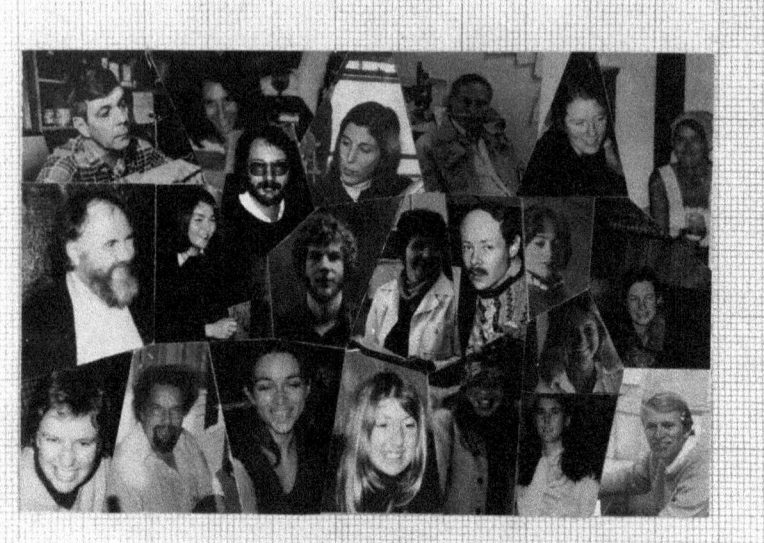

Collage of Bigelow Lab's regulars on Leonie's graph paper placemat. Top left to bottom right: Jack Laird, Carmen Sapienza, Randy King, Carrie Lewis, Charlie Yentsch, Susan Sykes, Sue Murray, Ian Morris, Sherry Hanson, Dave Phinney, Clarice Yentsch, Jerry Topinka, Andy Smith, Betsy Bass, Gretchen Hull, Lee Doggett, Chris Garside, Linda Sapienza, Hilary Bartlett, Rhonda Selvin, Jean Garside, Peter Larsen. 1980. Jim Rollins.

Chris Garside was seated at the Dory Bar. I was on one side and Donna Callnan, a hairdresser, on the other.

Chris said to me, "The trouble with the States is . . ."

Donna Callnan turned to his Nibs, "If you don't like it here, why don't you go home?" she said sharply. Bobby Rice, behind the bar, chuckled.

That conversation inspired me. I paid taxes, I wanted to have a say. I applied to become a U.S. citizen.

LEONIE BOWS OUT (1981-1982)

June Campbell Rose ran into the Thistle late one night in tears. She grabbed Kay Brown's arm. "Oh, Kay, John Lennon's just been shot."

"I'll never forget that moment," Kay said. "All of us were mourning together in the pub, especially June."

That tragedy marked a turning point at the Thistle. Danny Beal still played on Wednesday nights but Leonie struggled to make a profit and innovated. Happy Hour started at three instead of four and dining rooms stayed open for an extra thirty minutes. To defer costs of new menus, Leonie scratched out old prices and scribbled in new ones by hand. A constant frown crossed her face and she cracked fewer jokes. She threatened to sell the inn. We were spooked by that.

Bobby Rice addressed his concerns to his workmate, Rhonda. "I think Leonie's serious this time. She went over finances with me."

Rhonda was involved in a science project on Cape Cod, Massachusetts, during the week and came back to Boothbay to bartend on weekends. Alone in a cabin near Woods Hole one weeknight, Rhonda had written a heartfelt note about how much the Thistle Inn meant to her and sent it to Leonie.

Leonie dabbed her eyes after she read Rhonda's words.

Rhonda drove up to Boothbay on the next Friday afternoon to bartend at the Thistle that night.

"SURPRISE!" everyone cried when she came in and found a party in her honor. Leonie called for silence and read her letter out loud.

Bobby turned to Rhonda, "I didn't think you had that in you, kid."

Leonie's health deteriorated, she was in and out of the hospital. She became overwrought and said it was the end, but like a relentless tide she swept back in time after time.

Strohn Woodard was convinced he would never hear from her again. He wrote a sincere letter to her at Maine Medical Center in Portland saying he was sorry she would not be able to read it. He came in the Thistle a day or two later and there she was seated on her usual barstool, a glass of wine in hand. "So I said, 'Leonie, I've never known somebody who's dead and came back to life like you. What's it like? We all knew you were gone!'"

"I *was* gone," she said. "And it was the most wonderful experience. There was a light at the end of a tunnel. I was rushing to that light and I'd never been happier, ever. The thing that saved me was I'd read about this and knew what it meant. Turning around was the hardest thing I've ever done, but I turned around and came back. That's why I'm here."

"That was pretty impressive," Strohn said. "We had understood—you know the way people talk at the Thistle—all her organs had pretty much failed. She had real determination."

This notice appeared in the *Boothbay Register* on June 11th, 1981.

THE THISTLE INN

Open Year Round

All kinds of changes are going on here at Ye Olde Thistle. As of July we will be serving luncheon on our lovely porch, along with offering you a new imaginative menu. Also, June 21st will be our last day of keeping the bar open on Sunday for the summer season. There are plenty of places open in the winter and unless it rains it just doesn't warrant staying open for food and drinks. However, the Inn will be covered for rooms. Getting practical in my later years.

Leonie sold the Thistle Inn in September 1981 to a fellow who owned a liquor store in San José, California. She threw a grand farewell party in the Harness Room. Charlie Yentsch, Bigelow Lab's executive director, gave a moving speech and raised a glass to toast Leonie.

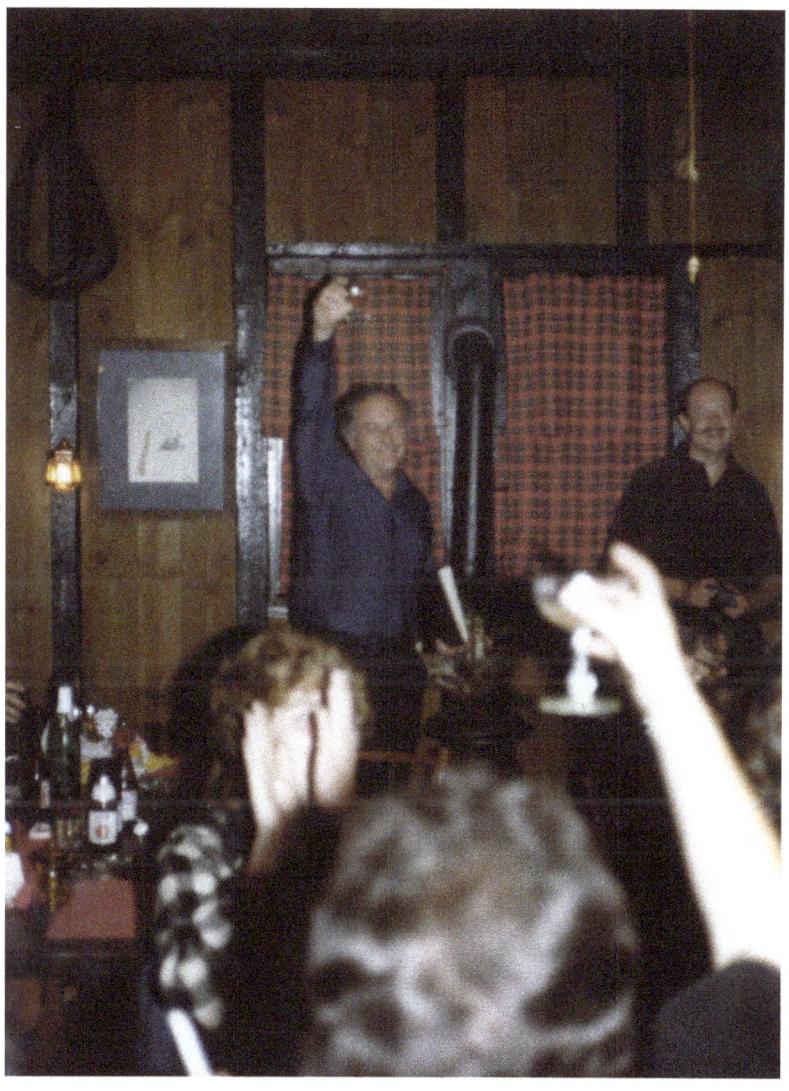

Charlie Yentsch (back left) toasts Leonie at her farewell party in the Harness Room. Jerry Topinka (back right) 1981. Hilary E. Bartlett

THE THISTLE INN

Open All Year

A lot of thought has been given to how I should write my last ad, and it still comes up with my first thought which is I hate writing it. It is like giving up your baby. Selling the Inn is the hardest thing I've ever done but it is a necessity. My health was the first consideration and with today's economic pressure, the endless paperwork, there was no way I could hack it alone as I have for the past fourteen years.

It is impossible to describe the love that has gone into the Inn, which is a home away from home for many, or for the love I feel for the people that have worked with me. And for my wonderful, wonderful customers (with a few exceptions) who have made it possible for me to serve the town on a year 'round basis, my gratitude is boundless.

I'd also like to thank the merchants in this town who have cooperated with me through bad and good times.

I have loved living here and although my home will be in Southport I shall always be interested in what is happening in Boothbay Harbor. Letters to the Editor this week!

The new owner is a very pleasant man who is concerned in maintaining the Inn as it is and certainly interested in catering to the natives. We are working together to make the transition period as pleasant as possible and I do hope everyone will come to meet him and wish him well. I wouldn't have sold to anyone that I thought wouldn't keep his word, and while you might find him introverted as much as I am extroverted, he has a wonderful dry sense of humor, which as I told him, he has to have to survive this crazy business.

The spirit of T'Donald, Bonnie and Robbie Burns join me in saying "Goodbye" and I hope the hell you miss my ads as much as I will miss writing them.

Lots and lots of love, Leonie

Leonie intended to write a book about her experiences at the Thistle Inn, but never had the opportunity. She collapsed and was taken to St. Andrews Hospital in Boothbay Harbor. Randy King from Bigelow Lab sat vigil at her bedside. Leonie died on May 7th, 1982. She was fifty-nine. Her resting place, next to T'Donald's in Boothbay's Evergreen Cemetery, is marked by a single word on a stone plaque, 'Leonie'.

I phoned Bigelow pals who lived out of state to give them the news. We mourned. Her death was the end of an era.

"She was very committed to Boothbay Harbor," her niece, Nadeen, said. "She was very opinionated in her expressing herself about it, of course, but you really heard her genuine desire for it to be successful. It wasn't that she wanted to prove that she was better or anything. It's just that she wanted people to be able to pull up their britches and make it all work. And so I think her years were very happily spent here."

Leonie had helped to organize the Boothbay Playhouse, a summer stock theater, and devoted hours to Red Cross work, the American Cancer Society and other charities. One summer she arranged a softball match between the Thistle Inn and the Rusty Anchor restaurant to raise funds for Boothbay Region Scholarship Fund. Leonie was a town selectman for Boothbay Harbor from 1977 to 1980. She declined to run for a second term because of poor health. Over the years she acted as director, president and secretary of Boothbay Region Chamber of Commerce. Leonie also served as chairman of promotion for Maine Innkeepers Association.

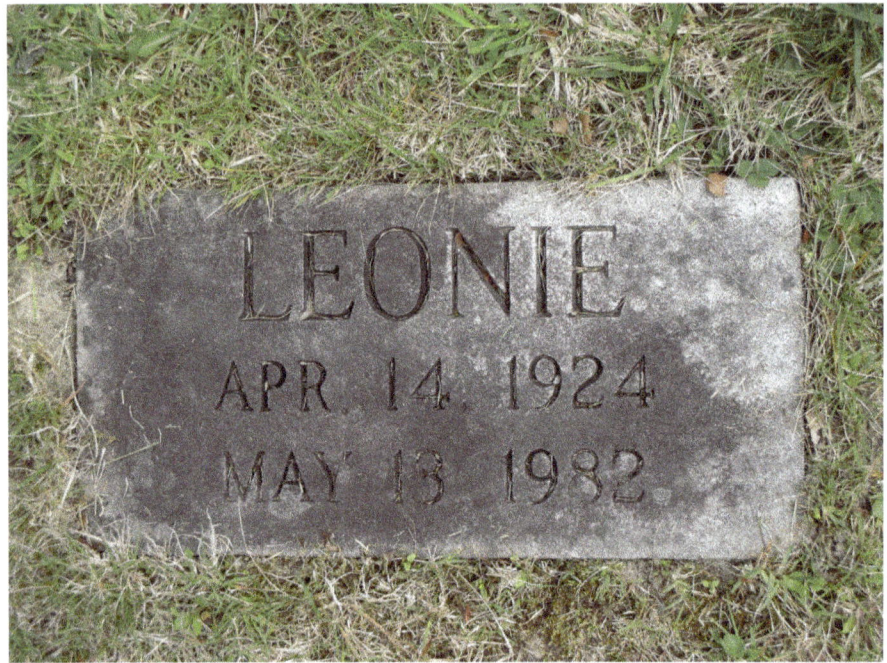

Headstone for Leonie Greenwood-Adams. 2018. Hilary E. Bartlett.

But mostly she will be remembered as owner of the Thistle Inn, which she managed for eighteen years. You have to like the human race to run a place like that and Leonie loved people.

The late Danny Beal, at one of his last local concerts, dedicated this song from *Les Misérables* to Leonie.

'There's a grief that can't be spoken

There's a pain goes on and on.

Empty chairs at empty tables

Now my friends are dead and gone . . . . .'

Mary Brewer, managing editor of the *Boothbay Register,* summed her up in a column opposite the innkeeper's obituary.

"Leonie. She was known to nearly everyone on a first-name basis. You never had to ask 'Leonie who?' You knew who they meant. Many words could be used to describe her. Outspoken. Intelligent. Sensitive. A fighter. Kind-hearted. Fun-loving. Stubborn. Trusting. In love with her community and her Inn.

"She was all of these, and more. She put her whole heart into everything she did, including her term as Town Selectman and her many years in the Region Chamber of Commerce. She sincerely loved the town and wanted it preserved and protected, and would willingly fight tooth and nail with anyone she disagreed with. She was not above name calling or cursing if it seemed appropriate. She had a big heart, with a soft spot for anyone down on his or her luck. Many people never really understood her and some never accepted her. Those who had the opportunity to talk at length with her, work with her or to serve on committees with her, realized she was a highly sensitive, intelligent, aware individual who lived her life unafraid of what others might think or say.

"She had requested no funeral. She didn't want her friends to mourn. In fact, she didn't really ask that they remember her, but that lady stamped a place for herself in the Boothbay Region that will always be hers, and hers alone."

A NEW ERA (1982-present)

Over the following decades owners came and went and the Thistle Inn had as many ups and downs as hemlines. Most of Leonie's regulars left.

Patricia Royall, a local gal and executive director of Boothbay Region Chamber of Commerce, spoke of the Thistle Inn after Leonie sold out. "I think the thing that was sad for me when it started to go through onerous times was the loss of community, because we always had a place and all of a sudden that place didn't feel the same."

Patricia encouraged the Reids to take over the Thistle Inn after it closed in August 2016. Dick was excited. Anya had misgivings. She had worked there on and off for fourteen years and was familiar with the long hours it took to run an inn. Plus they had a young baby. They seesawed back and forth for weeks until they went to a family barbeque near Augusta. Dick pulled off to park behind a line of cars on a country road and when Anya opened her door she was smacked by a gigantic thistle. "I threw my hands up and looked at him," she said with a laugh. "And we just knew we had do it — it was a sign."

They took a lease out that September and lived on site. Dick's parents and godmother helped them paint and spruce up the inn. "It's always been a special place for me," Anya said. "I've cleaned every inch of this building and been involved in pretty much all of the operation. The thing that I really enjoyed was meeting guests from all over the world. They come here and fall in love with the charm and history of this place." The new proprietors threw an opening party for the town on November 9th, 2016. "It was wall to wall people," Dick said. "And after Anya said something I hopped up on a bench and everyone's looking and I said, 'Welcome home - welcome back.' " Dick's message was powerful with locals. The Thistle Inn soon became one of the busiest restaurants in Boothbay Harbor.

Anya added, "I think part of why people have been so accepting is that I've bartended everywhere. I've been here a long time and made personal relationships and Dick was a staple in the community. I think our mindset is geared towards not, this is what we're doing, it's more, what would you like us to do for you? We're trying to find that balance where people can eat steak tips at a reasonable price and then anyone who wants to order a two hundred and fifty dollar bottle of wine can."

The Reids have embraced the Thistle's roots and want their tavern to reflect that history. They rummaged through attics and old painted signs are once more on display. Dick found a wooden billy club carved with images of Native Americans and Anya unearthed a piece of calligraphy, lost for thirty-eight years. The new proprietors are convinced the Thistle Inn is haunted by a mysterious man. Maybe the first owner of the house, lost at sea in 1863.

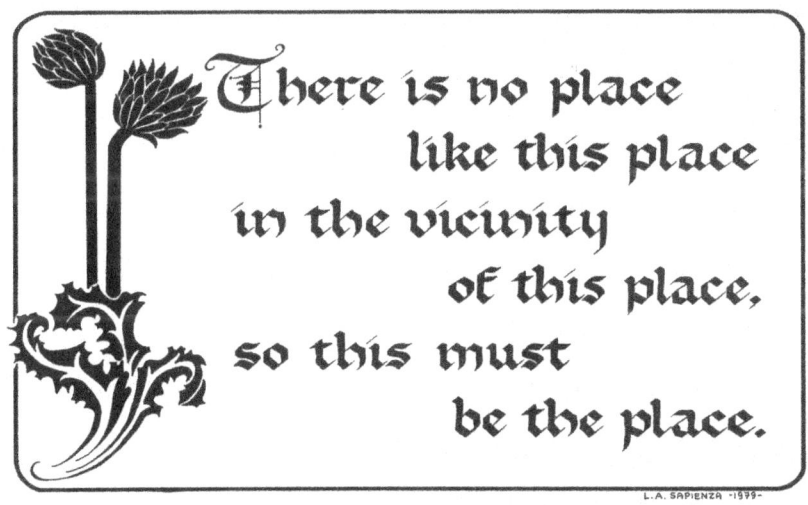

Calligraphy. 1979. Linda Sapienza. (Courtesy of Dick and Anya Reid)

"I love the fact that Dick and Anya have brought the place back," Patricia Royall said. "Part of the magic is it looks the same. Some of the seating has changed a little bit, but when you go in there it still feels like forty years ago. Leonie would have been happy."

The Thistle Inn now boasts a three-star hotel rating. Thanks to culinary awards—first place at 2017 Boothbay Harbor Fest, Best of the Fest, 2018, and voted #4 for Top 10 Best Hotel Restaurants in America (*USA TODAY*, 2019)—their reputation has soared. Up to this date they have been successful. The Dory Bar is busy at Happy Hour on winter nights, dining rooms are full and people have booked rooms for a summer vacation by the sea.

CONCLUSION

These days, when I kayak around Burnt Island, I am reminded of those early summer mornings in the mid-seventies that made me fall in love with Boothbay Harbor. Osprey swoop through a cloudless sky and call to their mates, golden sunbeams hit the lighthouse and a briny tang tickles my nose as I paddle along. A seal's whiskered face pops out of the water as if to say, "Hi!" Everything about this place grabs me, still.

The Bigelow sisters spent only three years together in the 1970s, yet the love that binds is strong. They are my American family. We tighten ranks when times are tough and celebrate with gusto. We reminisce about the time when we all lived in town and went to Happy Hour at the Thistle.

Linda Sapienza and I were in Santa Fe, New Mexico, eighteen years after Leonie died. We popped into a courtyard restaurant for lunch and talked about the Thistle's glory days – one of our favorite topics.

Linda suddenly grabbed my arm. "It's her."

"Who?"

"Leonie."

"Don't be daft."

"No, really! Don't look round she's coming this way."

I caught a whiff of Leonie's perfume when an older woman walked by with two male companions. Back towards me, she had on a cream fedora and matching pants topped with a long-sleeved tangerine jacket. She took a table a few yards away, sat and faced me.

"Can you see her?" Linda whispered.

"Holy Cow! You're right, she looks just like her. Maybe Leonie had a twin sister?"

I stared at the woman. Her eyes met mine. I flushed. "Come on Linda, we've got to go over." We introduced ourselves. I apologized for staring and gave her the low-down on Leonie.

"Well," she said, "sounds like a woman after my own heart. I'm an actress and I've been married several times. Why don't you join us?"

Leonie lives on through our stories, in a stranger's face, and a hint of familiar perfume.

BIBLIOGRAPHY

Australian Dictionary of Biography, "Caron Leon Francis Victor (1805-1905)" Volume 3. 1969. https://www.adb.edu.au/biography/caron-leon-francis-victor-3167.

Boothbay Register archives; 1963 to 2018.

Bureau of Highway Safety, "Historical Timeline for Maine's OUI Laws," 2016. https:www.aone.gov/dps/bhs/impaired-driving facts.html

Clifford, Harold B. *The Boothbay Harbor Region 1906-1960.* Freeport Maine, the Bond Wheelright Company, 1961.

Falkowski, Paul, ed. *Primary Productivity in the Sea.* New York, Plenum Press, 1980.

Greene, Byron Francis. *History of Boothbay. Southport and Boothbay Harbor.* Somersworth New Hampshire, New England History Press, 1984.

Leaf, Earl and Leonie Greenwood-Adams, "Haitian Hoedown," *Colliers Weekly,* May 4, 1946. 22-29.

"Man May Learn a Lot From Pigs," *Iola Register,* January 31, 1977.

Maine Department of Resources, *A Guide to Lobstering in Maine,* Augusta, Maine, 2005.

"Massive Bluefin Tuna Rakes in $323,000 at Tsukiji Market Auction," January 5th, 2018. https://www.eater.com/2018/1/516853698/tsukiji-tuna-auction-2018-japan.

"Meet Earl Leaf," *Popular Photography,* December, 1947. p 261.

National Fisherman, "Small Draggers Live off Whiting in Summer." August, 1968. https://www.nationalfisherman.com/archive/from-the-nf-archives-the-american-fisherman-august-1968/.

Rice, George Wharton. *The Shipping Days of Old Boothbay.* Somersworth New Hampshire, New England History Press and Boothbay Region Historical Society, 1984.

Rumsey, Barbara. *Boothbay Region Historical Sketches* Volume II. Boothbay Maine, Boothbay Region Historical Society, 1999.

The Scotsman, "True Scotsmen are told to cover-up," February 15, 2009. https://www.scotsman.com 1-829419.

Woodard, Colin. *The Lobster Coast: Rebels, Rusticators, and the Struggle for a Forgotten Frontier.* New York, Penguin Books, 2004.

APPENDICES

1. Regional Map

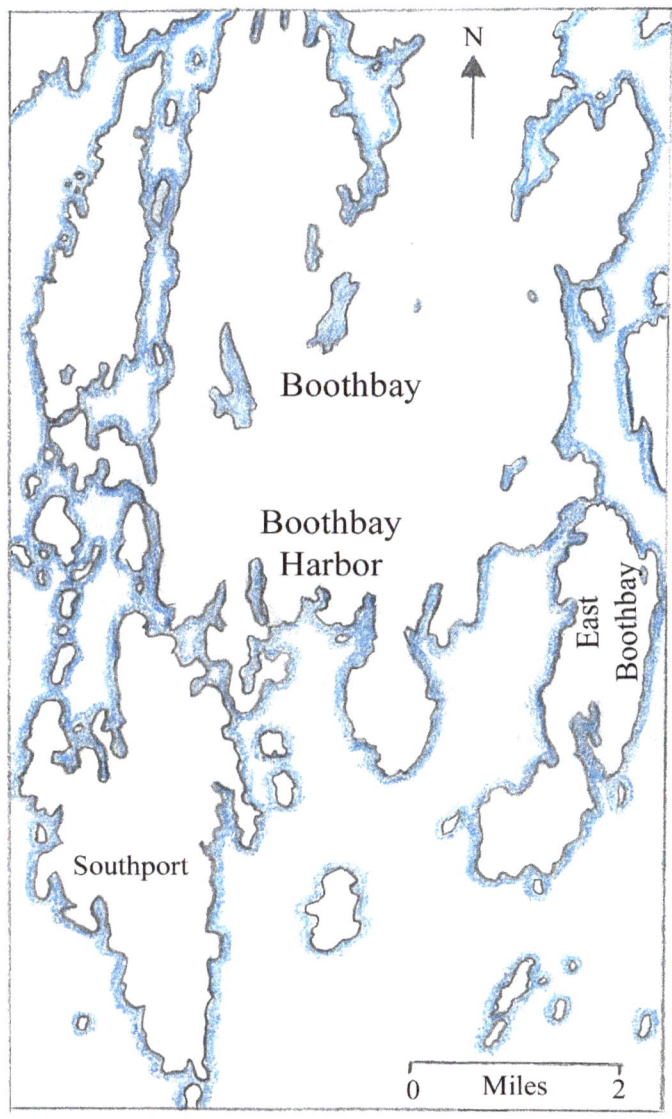

Region map redrawn from Sheepscot Valley Conservation Association GIS Support Center, 2015. Hilary E. Bartlett (Courtesy of Boothbay Region Chamber of Commerce)

2. Downtown Boothbay Harbor Map 1963 – 1981

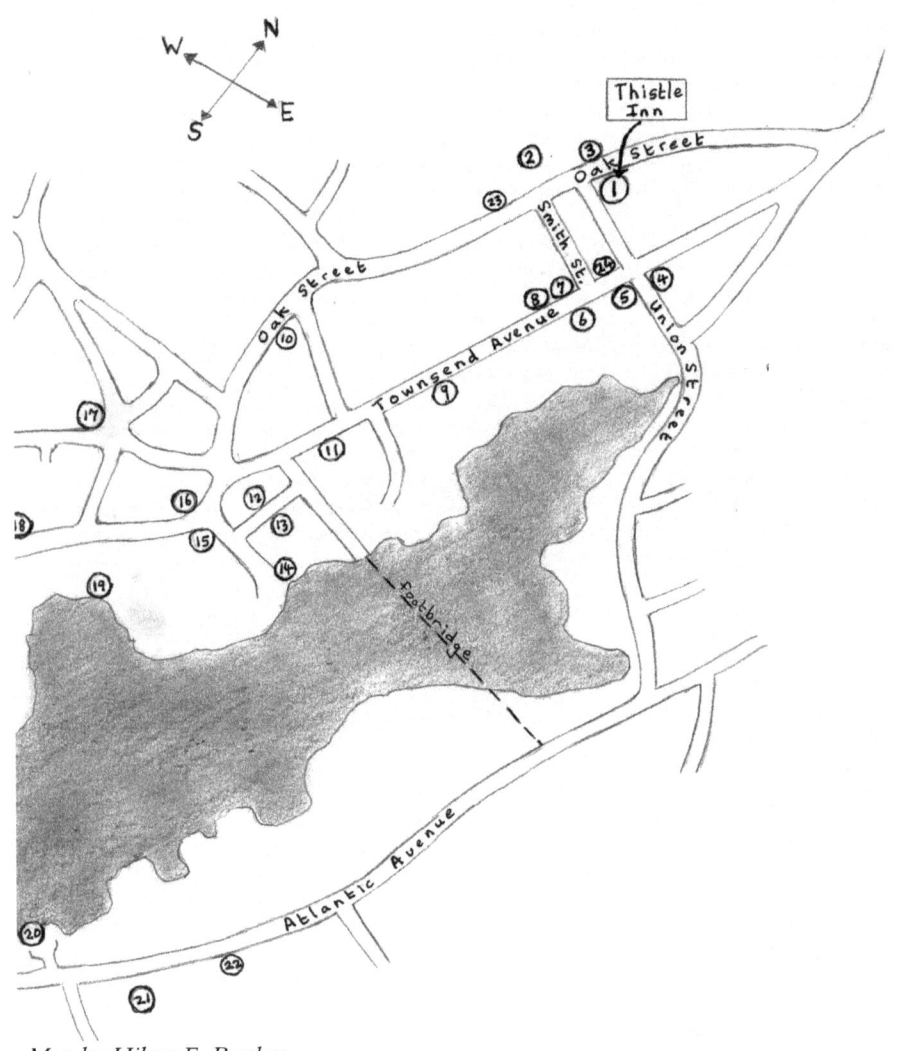

Map by Hilary E. Bartlett

(1) Thistle Inn
(2) My house
(3) Oliver Stratton's
(4) Boothbay Register
(5) Wheeler's Drug Store
(6) United First Methodist Church
(7) Opera House
(8) Strand Movie Theater [burnt down, 1982]
(9) Grover's Hardware
(10) Post Office
(11) Porter's Drug Store
(12) Irene's Café
(13) Romar Bowling Lanes
(14) McSeagull's [was Robins' Luncheonette]
(15) Carbone's Market
(16) Orne's Candy Store
(17) Police Station
(18) Ebbtide Restaurant
(19) Public Town Landing
(20) Malpeque Shrimps Plant [closed 1970s]
(21) Catholic Church
(22) Freezer [burnt down, 1978]
(23) Harbor Travel
(24) Mac Andrews Gulf Station

Townsend Avenue heads north (off map) to Finast Supermarket and Boothbay Region Schools.

3. 1885 Map

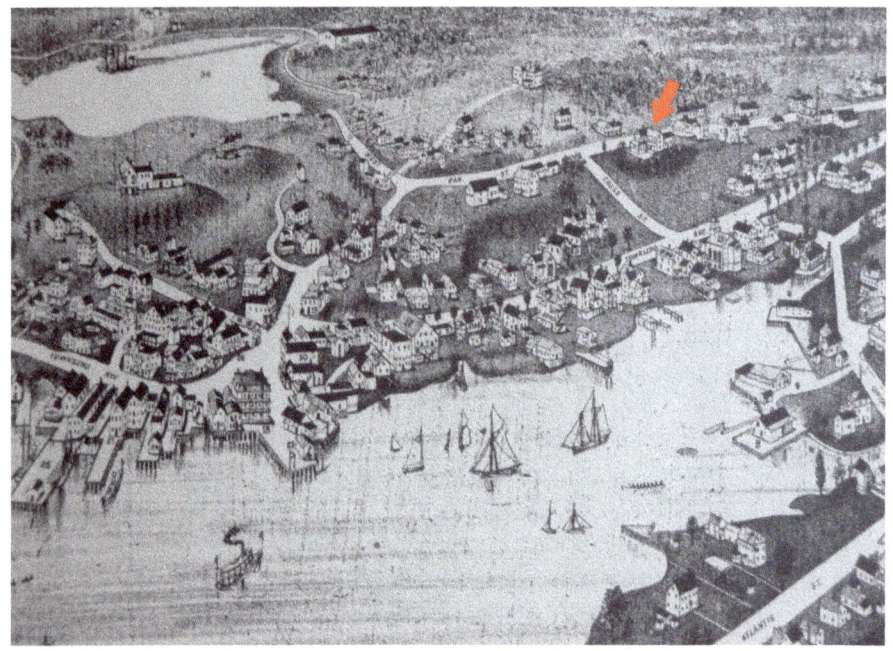

Section of 1885 map of Boothbay Harbor. Captain Reed's house is on Oak Street (red arrow). (Courtesy of Boothbay Region Historical Society)

4. T'Donald's Obituary

(BOOTHBAY REGISTER, November 23rd, 1967)

Donald B. Morren of Thistle Inn Dies Suddenly

Donald Booth Morren of Boothbay Harbor died suddenly at his home on November 21st at the age of forty-one. He was the owner and operator of the Thistle Inn, "A Wee Bit of Scotland in Maine."

He was born in Edinburgh, Scotland on July 21, 1926, the son of Sir William and Lady Evelyn Morren.

He came to this country in 1954 and opened the Thistle Inn here in July of 1963. He was a graduate of Melville College in Edinburgh, and a member of Holyrood House St. Luke's No. 44 Masonic Lodge of Edinburgh.

Survivors include his wife, Leonie Greenwood-Adams Morren of Boothbay Harbor, his father and mother of Edinburgh, one son, Michael of England, a sister, Miss Evelyn Morren of Edinburgh, and a brother, Gordon, of London, England.

Funeral services will be held Saturday, November 25th at 2:30 p.m. at the Boothbay Congregational Church with Rev. Balmforth officiating. Burial will be in Evergreen Cemetery, Boothbay.

5. Top Section of 1966 Menu Cover

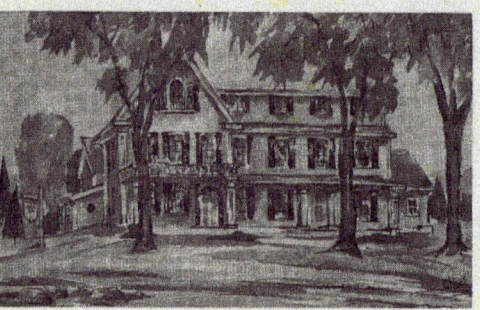

(Courtesy of Boothbay Region Historical Society)

6. 1966 Menu

Luncheon

TASTE BUD TEASERS

Our Original Fish Clam Chowder...	Cup	.45
....	Bowl	.90
Ice Cold Highland Tattie Creamed Soup...		.45
Soup de Jour..		.40
Chilled Juices...		.25
Fruit Cocktail with Sherbet..		.45

ENTREES

Maine Steamed lobster with drawn butter, lemon wedge with homemade Edinburgh style potato salad...	3.50
Broiled Fresh Fish of the Day...	1.85
Ooour own lobster salad with chunks of succulent lobster on crisp lettuce garnished with tomato wedges and imported olives............................	2.50
Broiled or deep fried scallops with potato salad..	2.50
Frrresh Maine crabmeat salad on crisp lettuce with tomato wedges and Spanish Olives...	2.00
Garden Fresh Tossed Green Salad Bowl with Potato Chips........................	.90
Special Fruit Salad with Cottage Cheese with all the garnishes..................	1.50

All above entrees served with hot rolls and butter

SANDWICHES

Leonie's toasted Maine lobster roll, filled to overflowing, garnished with tomato wedges and Spanish Olives..	2.00
Toasted Maine crabmeat roll served with crisp lettuce, pickles and potato crisps...........	1.50
4 to 5 oz. freshly ground beef hamburger on a bun garnished with lettuce, pickles and potato crisps..	.80
With Cheese.......................................	.90
Ham or Turkey on choice of breads, potato crisps and pickles...................	.75
With Cheese.......................................	.85
Ooour own Robbie Burns Steak Sandwich with lettuce, tomato and potato salad	1.85
Grilled Cheese sandwich with potato chips and pickles............................	.65
Thistle Club sandwich with potato salad...	1.50
Open faced Roast Beef Sandwich with lettuce, tomato and Edinburgh style potato salad...	1.75

Side Order of Homemade Edinburgh style potato salad 30 cents

AFTERS AND BEVERAGES . . . SEE DINNER MENU

Dinner

TASTE BUD TEASERS

Our Original Fish Clam Chowder...	Cup	.45
....	Bowl	.90
Ice Cold Highland Tattie Creamed Soup...		.45
Soup de Jour..		.40
Chilled Juices...		.25
Fruit Cocktail with Sherbet..		.45

ENTREES

Our Own Lobster Salad
    with chunks of succulent lobster on crisp lettuce fully garnished....................... $2.75
Leonie's Crabmeat Salad $2.25

	Full Dinner	A la Carte
Our Specialty — T'Donald's Scottish Lobster Pie		
Chunks of lobster removed from the shell sautéed in butter and combined with a sauce of mushrooms, spices and two different sherry wines . . . then gently baked in a casserole with flaky crust........................	4.75	4.00
Lazy Lobster	4.75	4.00
Live Boiled Lobster		
Served with the potato of your choice and drawn butter........................	4.75	4.00
Baked Stuffed Lobster		
Served with the potato of your choice and drawn butter........................	4.95	4.25
Roast Beef		
Juicy and tender — served verra, verra rare to well done outside cuts	4.85	4.00
Our own Robbie Burns Steak		
Tender, succulent prime steer seasoned and broiled to your preference........	3.75	3.25
Thicker Cut...	4.75	4.25
Rare – done outside, cool center.		
Medium Rare – done outside, warm center.		
Medium – done through, pink hot center.		
We canna be responsible for steaks cooked beyond the medium point!		
Kingdom of Fife Pie		
Breasts of turkey and chicken baked in our special white sauce with herbs and flaky crust...	3.50	2.75
Broiled Fresh Fish of the Day...,...	2.85	2.25
Fish and Chips		
Filet of fresh fish breaded and deep fried to a golden brown, served with crisp French Fries...	2.50	1.75

	Full Dinner	A la Carte
Broiled Bay Scallops a la Francaise		
Tender scallops broiled in the shell with a verra delicate Sherry Butter Sauce	3.00	2.50
Baked Stuffed..	3.50	3.00
Breaded Butterfly Gulf Shrimp		
Crisply fried with tartar sauce and lemon wedge..	3.00	2.50
All full dinners include appetizer, vegetable, hot rolls "afters" and coffee.		
SPECIAL:		
1,000 Island Spring Rainbow Trout. Broiled to perfection in butter with potatoes and vegetables..	3.95	3.50

VEGETABLES   (A la Carte — all .35)

Fresh Vegetables of the Day (In Season)
Baked, French Fried or Mashed Potatoes

Crisp Garden Fresh Tossed Salad... .45

Special Salad Dressings — Ask the Lassies

AFTERS

Scottish Sherry Trifle (10 cents extra on dinner)..	.50
Indian Pudding with Ice Cream (10 cents extra on dinner)..................................	.50
Home Made Pie of the Day...	.40
Various Ice Creams and Sherbets...	.35
4 Layer White Cake with Hot Butterscotch sauce...	.45
Tart of the Day..	.40

BEVERAGES

Thistle Inn Coffee...	.15	(Iced .20)
English Tea..	.15	(Iced .20)
Milk...	.20	
Sanka...	.20	

Have a second cup of ooour Coffee "On the Hoose"!

If ye be in a hurry, may we suggest trying another of this wee town's eatin' establishments.

ALL PRICES INCLUDE 4% MAINE STATE TAX

From The Dory

T'Donald's Specials $1.00

Robbie Burns Cocktail
Scottish Mule (Scotch and
 Schweppes ginger beer)
Irish Mule (Irish and
 Schweppes ginger beer)
Mexican Mule (Tequila and
 Schweppes ginger beer)
Moscow Mule (Vodka and
 Schweppes ginger beer)

COCKTAILS

Beefeater Martini	.95
Martini	.90
Manhattan	.90
Whiskey Sour	.90
Bloody Mary	.90
Old Fashioned	.90
Daiquiri	.90
Gibson	.90
Sidecar	1.00
Stinger	1.00
Bacardi	.90
Rob Roy	.95
Gin Alexander	1.00
Brandy Alexander	1.00
Grasshopper	1.00
Champagne Cocktail	1.50
Jack Rose	.90
Fizzes	.90

SCOTCH WHISKEYS

Thistle Scotch	1.00
Haig & Haig Pinch Bottle	1.00
Johnnie Walker Black Label	1.00
Chivas Regal	1.00
Grants "8"	.95
J & B	.95
Cutty Sark	.95
Dewar's White Label	.95

Leonie's Specials $1.00

Rusty Nail (Scotch and Drambuie)
Thistle Rob Roy (Scotch, Dry
 Vermouth and Drambuie)
Black Russian (Vodka and Tia Maria)
The Boomerang (Milk, Scotch and
 Crème de Cacao)

BOURBON WHISKEYS

Jack Daniels Black	.95
I. W. Harper	.95
Jack Daniels Green	.95
Old Grand Dad	.95
Old Fitzgerald	.95
Old Forester	.95
Early Times	.85
Old Crow	.85
Jim Beam	.85
Bellow's Club	.85
J. W. Dant – 12 yr.	.85
Bar Whiskey	.80

GINS

Beefeater	.90
Booth's House of Lords	.90
DeKuyper Geneva Gin	.85
Seagram's Extra Dry	.85
Gordon's	.85
Gilby's	.85
Poland Spring Sloe Gin	.85
Bar Gin	.80

VODKAS

Smirnoff No. 57	.90
Smirnoff No. 21	.85
Fleischmann's	.85
Bar Vodka	.80

SCOTCH WHISKEYS

Teacher's	.95
100 Pipers	.95
King William IV	.95
Inver House	.95
Martin's V.V.O.	.95
Ballantine's	.95
Black & White	.95
Black & White Ex Light	.95
Haig & Haig Five Star	.95
Johnnie Walker Red Label	.95
White Horse	.95
Vat 69	.95
King George	.95
Bar Scotch	.90

CANADIAN WHISKEYS

Seagram's Crown Royal	1.00
Schenley O.F.C.	1.00
Canadian Club	1.00
Seagram's V.O.	.90
Canadian Lord Calvert	.90
Black Velvet	.90
Allen's	.90
McNaughton's	.90

BLENDED WHISKEYS

Seagram's 7 Crown	.85
Four Roses	.85
Schenley Reserve	.85
Imperial	.85
Fleischmann's	.85
Bellow's Reserve	.85
Bellow's Partner's Choice	.85
Calvert	.85
Bar Whiskey	.80
★ ★ ★	
John Jameson (Irish)	.85
Kennedy's (Irish)	.85
Old Overholt (Straight Rye)	.85

RUMS

Old Medford Demarara	.85
Hudson Bay – Demarara	.85
Bar Rum	.80
Meyer's Jamaican	.85
Bacardi	.85
Caldwell's Demarara	.85

COOLING DRINKS

Sloe Gin Fizz	.90
Pink Wink	.90
Collins	.90
Ward Eight	.90
Gin and Schweppes	.90
Screwdriver	.90
Singapore Sling	.95
Planter's Punch	.95

BRANDIES

	Pony
Courvoisier	.90
Hennessy 3 Star	.90
Martell	.90
Christian Brothers	.85
Laird's Apple	.85
Arrow Apricot	.85
Arrow Blackberry	.85
Old Mr. Boston Cherry	.85

CORDIALS and LIQUEURS

	Pony
Galliano	1.00
Irish Mist	1.00
Drambuie	1.00
Grand Marnier	1.00
B & B	1.00
Benedictine	1.00
Cherry Heering	1.00
Green Chartreuse	1.00
Yellow Chartreuse	1.00
Tia Maria	1.00
Cointreau	1.00
Crème de Cacao	.75
Crème de Menthe	.75
Anisette	.75

WINES BEFORE DINNER

Sherry (Domestic)	.50
Duff Gordon (Imported)	.70
Dubonnet	.60

WINES WITH DINNER

RED WINES	Glass	Bottle
Chateauneuf-du-Pape, La Bernadine	.55	5.00
Chianti	.50	4.50
Beaujolais	.50	4.50
Nectarose	.50	4.50
Grand Cru Tavel	.50	4.00
Haut Medoc	.50	4.00
Taylor's Rose	.50	3.50
Taylor's Burgundy	.50	3.50
Lancer's – Bott		
Lancer's – Split		

WHITE WINES	Glass	Bottle
Liebfraumilch – Blue Nun	.55	5.00
Pouilly Fuise Latour	.55	5.00
Sauterne, A. DeLuze & Fils	.50	4.50
Sauterne (Domestic)	.50	3.00
Almaden Chablis	.50	3.00
Paul Masson (Split)		2.00

AFTER DINNER WINES

Sherry	.50
Port	.50
Muscatel	.50
Harvey's Bristol Cream	.90

CHAMPAGNE

Piper Heidsick – Vintage	14.00
Piper Heidsick Extra Dry	13.00
Mumm's Extra Dry	13.00
Moet & Chandon	13.00
Great Western Extra Dry	7.00
Taylor's	7.00
Taylor's Pink	7.00

SPARKLING BURGUNDY

Great Western	7.00
Taylor's	7.00

BEER and ALE

A Blimey (Roses Lime and beer)	.50
A Yard of Beer or Ale	2.00
Draught	1.50

Imported

Guiness Stout	.75
Bass Ale	.75
Heinekin	.75
Tuborg	.75
Carlsberg	.75
Lowenbrau (light or dark)	.75

Domestic

Miller	.45
Schlitz	.45
Budweiser	.45
Schaefer	.45
Narragansett	.45
Ballentine Ale	.45
Michelob	.65
Draught Millers	.40

ALL PRICES INCLUDE 4 % MAINE STATE TAX

(Courtesy of Boothbay Region Historical Society)

7. 1978 Menu

Luncheon

TASTE BUD TEASERS

Fresh Lobster Stew..	Cup	2.50
....	Bowl	4.75
Fresh Fish Chowder..	Cup	.90
....	Bowl	1.75
Chilled Juices...		.50

ENTREES

Broiled Fresh Fish of the Day	4.00
Broiled or deep fried Scallops...	......
Chef Brock's Salad – Ham, Turkey, Swiss Cheese, American Cheese, Egg, Tomato Wedges, Cucumbers, Celery and Crisp Lettuce............................	4.00
Garden Fresh Tossed Green Salad Bowl..	2.00

All above entrees served with hot French bread and butter

SANDWICHES

Leonie's toasted Maine Lobster roll, filled to overflowing, garnished with tomato wedges and olives...	4.95
5 oz. freshly ground beef hamburger on a bun garnished with pickles and potato crisps...	1.75
with cheese...	1.85
Turkey or Ham Club Sandwich...	2.75
Ham and Cheese on choice of breads, potato crisps with pickles..............................	1.75
Ooour own Robbie Burns Steak Sandwich with lettuce, tomato and French Fries...	4.25
Fishwich Sandwich – Lightly fried fresh fish on roll Served with pickles and Crisps	3.00

Egg Salad Sandwich...	1.25
Grilled Cheese Sandwich with potato crisps and pickles.........................	.95
Side Order of French Fries..	.50

ASK THE LASSIES FOR SURPRISE SPECIALS

AFTERS

Scottish Sherry Trifle..	1.00
Indian Pudding with Ice Cream..	.95
Pie of the Day..	.75
Various Ice Creams and Sherbets	.50
2 Layer White Cake with Hot Butterscotch sauce	1.00
Cheesecake..	1.00

BEVERAGES

Thistle Inn Coffee	.50	(Iced .60)
Tea	.30	(Iced .35)
Milk		.75
Sanka		.30
Irish Coffee		2.00

Dinner

TASTE BUD TEASERS ... AFTERS AND BEVERAGES

SEE LUNCHEON MENU

ENTREES (Include potato and vegetable) — cooked to Order

Our Specialty – T'Donald's Scottish Lobster Pie
    Chunks of lobster removed from the shell, sautéed in butter and combined with a sauce of mushrooms, spices, sherry wine ... then baked in a casserole with flaky crust.. 8.50

Live 1¼ pound Boiled Lobster or Baked Stuffed Lobster
    Served with drawn butter   Boiled......................
    Served with Herb and Seafood Stuffing   Baked......................

Scallops Flambé
    Fresh scallops sautéed in onions, tomatoes, green peppers, mushrooms, flambéed in brandy, served on fluffy rice...

Broiled scallops a la Francaise
    Tender scallops broiled with a verra delicate Sherry Butter Sauce....................
    Baked Stuffed (Herb and Seafood)..

Fried Scallops..

Baked Haddie au Frommage
    Fresh fillet of haddock covered with Swiss cheese and Breadcrumbs and baked in Celery Soup.. 7.50

Baked Stuffed Fish – with Newburg sauce... 8.95

Fish and Chips
    Filet of fresh fish breaded and deep fried to a golden brown
    Served with crisp French Fries... 7.00

Broiled Fish of the Day.. 7.00

Our Justly Famous Robbie Burns Steak
    Tender, succulent prime steer seasoned and broiled to your preference (10 oz.).... 8.75

Down East Steak
    Ooour verra own version of superb steak smothered with a mushroom sauce
    filled with chunks of lobster.. 14.00

Chef's Specialty Steak
    Broiled to your desire and covered with sautéed peppers, onions,
    mushrooms and melted cheese... 8.95

Steak and Onions Scottish Farmhouse Style.. 8.95

Steak Tips — Sautéed in tantalizing Maitre d'hôtel sauce, with
    green peppers, mushrooms, onions and tomatoes................................... 7.50

Roast Beef
    Juicy and tender — served verra rare to well done outside cuts.................. 7.00
               (FRIDAY AND SATURDAY ONLY)

Kingdom of Fife Pie
    Breasts of turkey baked in our special white sauce
    with herbs and flaky crust.. 4.95

VEGETABLES
            Fresh vegetables of the Day (In Season) .50

Crisp Garden Fresh Tossed Salad.. .85

            Special Salad Dressings — ask the lassies

      ASK THE LASSIES FOR PRICES FOR CHILDREN UNDER 12

          All Prices Include 5% Maine Sales Tax

From The Dory

COCKTAILS

Galliano Specials	2.00
Thistle Rob Roy	1.95
Beefeater Martini	1.65
Gimlet	1.60
Brandy Alexander	1.85
Grasshopper	1.85
Rusty Nail	2.00
Black Russian	2.00
Singapore Sling	1.85
The Boomerang	1.95
Margarita	1.80
Sidecar	1.85
Stinger	1.85
Bacardi Cocktail	1.60
Rob Roy	1.70
Jack Rose	1.70
Whiskey Sour	1.60
Bloody Mary	1.60
Old Fashioned	1.60
Daiquiri	1.60
Gibson	1.60
Kahlua Sombrero	1.90
Sombrero	1.60
Martini	1.60
Manhattan	1.60
Tequila Sunrise	1.60
Harvey Wallbanger	2.00

SCOTCH WHISKEYS

Haig & Haig Pinch Bottle	1.80
Johnnie Walker Black Label	1.90
Chivas Regal	1.90
Johnnie Walker Red Label	1.75
J & B	1.75
Cutty Sark	1.75
Dewar's White Label	1.75
Teacher's	1.75
Martin's V.V.O.	1.75
100 Pipers	1.75
King William	1.75
Inver House	1.75

SCOTCH WHISKEYS

Ballantine's	1.75
Black & White	1.75
Haig & Haig Five Star	1.75
Scoresby Rare	1.75
Bar Scotch	1.70

CANADIAN WHISKEYS

Seagram's Crown Royal	1.90
Canadian Club	1.75
Seagram's V.O.	1.75
Schenley O.F.C.	1.75
Canadian Lord Calvert	1.75
Black Velvet	1.60
Canadian Mist	1.60

BLENDED WHISKEYS

Seagram's 7 Crown	1.60
Four Roses	1.60
Schenley Reserve	1.60
Fleishmann's	1.60
Calvert	1.60
Bar Whiskey	1.60

★ ★ ★

John Jameson (Irish)	1.80
Irish Coffee	2.00

BOURBON WHISKEYS

Wild Turkey	1.90
Jack Daniels Black	1.90
Old Grandad (86 proof)	1.75
Old Fitzgerald	1.75
Early Times	1.75
Jim Beam	1.75
Bar Bourbon	1.60

CORDIALS and LIQUEURS

Grand Marnier	2.00
B & B	2.00

GINS

Beefeater	1.75
Tanqueray	1.75
Seagram's Extra Dry	1.60
Gordon's	1.60
Poland Spring Sloe Gin	1.60
Bar Gin	1.60

VODKAS

Smirnoff (100 proof)	1.75
Smirnoff No 21 (80 proof)	1.75
Bar Vodka	1.60

RUMS

Mt. Gay	1.75
Myer's Jamaican	1.75
Bacardi	1.75
Bar Rum	1.60

COOLING DRINKS

Planter's Punch	1.95
Pimm's Cup	1.95
Sloe Gin Fizz	1.75
Ward Eight	1.75
Collins	1.60
Gin and Schweppes	1.60
Screwdriver	1.60
Wine Cooler	.90

BRANDIES

Courvoisier	2.00
Hennessey 3 Star	1.95
Laird's Apple	1.75
Christian Brothers	1.60
Arrow Apricot	1.60
Arrow Blackberry	1.60

CORDIALS and LIQUEURS

Galliano	2.00
Irish Mist	1.90
Drambuie	1.90
Benedictine	1.90
Cherry Heering	1.90
Tia Maria	1.90
Amaretto	1.90
Cointreau	1.75
Southern Comfort	1.75
Crème de Cacao	1.60
Crème de Menthe	1.60
Anisette	1.60
Pernod	1.90

WINES BEFORE DINNER

Sherry (Domestic)	1.00
Duff Gordon (Imported)	1.50
Dubonnet	1.50

AFTER DINNER WINES

	Glass
Sherry	1.00
Port	1.00
Harvey's Bristol Cream	1.65

For all other wines and champagnes see our Wine List

BEER and ALE

Draft	.70
Imported	
Heinekin	1.25
Guinness	1.25
Domestic	
Miller	.85
Schlitz	.85
Budweiser	.85
Pabst	.85
Lite	.85
Ballentine Ale	.85
Black Horse Ale	.85
Molson Ale	.85
Michelob	1.00

All Prices Include 5% Maine Sales Tax

(Courtesy of Dick and Anya Reid)

8. Leonie's Letter to the Editor

(*BOOTHBAY REGISTER*, January 8th, 1976)

Dear Editor:

Again I am turning to Letters to the Editor to discuss a subject that is of importance to the Boothbay Harbor Region . . . year round Class A Restaurant eating facilities.

From 1963 to 1973 (with the exception of a few months when we built on our new kitchen, pub and rooms) the Thistle Inn served full luncheons and dinners six days a week all year. From 1963 to 1967 with my late husband T'Donald in the kitchen, waitresses were paid $15.00 a week for 2 shifts, 6 days a week, the cost of food, fuel, etc. one half of what it is now and with no other restaurants except the Ledges open in the area, we broke even in winter.

After my husband died, the shrimp arrived, and with a chef in the kitchen, rising costs and competition, we still managed fairly well. But from 1970 on it went rapidly downhill and it became obvious that it meant losing money to stay open.

When the Tugboat decided to serve meals during the winter we heaved a sigh of relief and felt that they could take over the responsibility of serving the community during the winter months, but it did not take long for them to realize it was a money losing situation with their larger overhead and they closed. (It should be mentioned that Harold Jordan tried to stay open during the winter before the Thistle opened and found it unfeasible). So in 1975, at the request of many people, we said we would attempt it again. As promised we stayed open full-time until this week, but despite our loyal friends and in particular Bigelow Laboratories supporting us, we again cannot afford to remain open on a full-time basis and survive. Hence, the restricted dining schedule.

And now we get down to brass tacks, why is it impossible for a Class A Restaurant and Bar to serve luncheon and dinner during winter and not lose money?

FIRST AND FOREMOST, we are at the endless end of Route 27 subject to the weather's whims. Secondly, there is much more competition on Route 1. Thirdly, the town is dependent on fishing and boat building for its income 8 months of the year, and when the fish aren't there, and the economy is bad, we are a depressed area. Please remember this when you hear people knocking the tourist business because without it there would be nothing open in this town but a few basic requirement stores. Fourth, the high cost of living. Last, but not least, the percentage of the population who do support local restaurants is much lower than it should be. Putting aside the economic factor, many people automatically go out of town for eating and buying. And then there is a certain element, in my particular case, that do their best to prevent people from patronizing the Thistle Inn.

It is true that we have just gone through a most unpleasant hippie-drug period from which all of us have suffered, particularly a place like mine that caters to such a diversified clientele. But that is the name of the game and you make the best of it. We certainly are not perfect, and like any restaurant have some bad days, but we do try to serve you the best at reasonable prices.

It all really comes down to working together when the going is tough. Competition is healthy, and I'm all for it, but not when there isn't enough business for even one to survive . . . putting the restaurant business aside; just look at the local motel situation. There is much more to be said, and debated I'm sure, but in the meantime, we shall continue to do our very best to be of service to the community, and with all our hearts we thank those who have remained faithful over the years and to those more newly arrived in the area who have supported us to the best of their economic ability.

Perhaps returning to the barter system for all of us is the best solution!

Optimistically yours,

Leonie Greenwood-Adams

9. Leonie's Obituary

(BOOTHBAY REGISTER, May 13th, 1982)

Leonie H. Greenwood-Adams, 59, of Southport, former Thistle Inn owner, Boothbay Harbor selectman, and Region Chamber of Commerce President, died Friday May 7 at St. Andrews Hospital. She was born April 14, 1924, in New York City, daughter of Marmion P. Greenwood-Adams and Irma T. Caron, and was educated in Flushing New York Schools and at a business college on Long Island.

A summer visitor here in the region since childhood, she and her late husband, T'Donald Morren, purchased the Thistle Inn in 1963. She operated it until 1981 when she sold the business.

A former free-lance professional writer and photographer, she had worked for Pan American World Airways, the *Sydney Morning Herald* in Australia, *Time* Magazine, *Colliers*, *Holiday* and others.
She also worked as an Executive Secretary for Blair Advertising agencies and the British Automobile Society. She had also devoted a great deal of time to volunteer Red Cross work. Here in the Boothbay Region, she had served as a director, president and secretary for the Boothbay Region Chamber of Commerce, had served as chairman of promotion for Maine Innkeepers Association, as a Boothbay Harbor selectman, and had done a great deal of volunteer work for the American Cancer Society and other charities.

Surviving are a half-brother, Leon C. Enge of Lafayette, Colorado and Nadeen Reinecke of Denver, Colorado.

Private services will be held at the convenience of the family.

An open house is planned for Sunday, May 16th from 2-4 p.m. at Leonie's cottage, East Shore Road, Southport, (near All Saints-by-the-Sea Church) hosted by the family.

Friends who wish to make donations in Leonie's name to the Boothbay Harbor Memorial Library Children's Room, or to a charity of their own choice.

ABOUT THE AUTHOR

Hilary E. Bartlett was born and raised in Liverpool, England with belching chimneys, street gangs and perpetual damp. When the Beatles first played at the Cavern she was there, but that was as good as it got. Good grades were her means of escape. Hilary studied microbiology at University College London and received her doctorate. She came to Bigelow Laboratory in Midcoast Maine in her late twenties to determine a predictive index for toxic red tides. Her intention was to return to London but Boothbay Harbor bewitched her. She took a full-time research position at Bigelow Lab and lived opposite the Thistle Inn during the 1970s. Hilary made life-long friends at the back corner table in the pub, where Bigelow sisters first shared stories about feisty grandmothers. Those young women changed Hilary's life. Yet she was the only one who stayed in Boothbay Harbor. Once she found her true home, she never wanted to leave.

Hilary changed careers after she became a mother and started a home-based art business. Her reputation as an artist is well established and her ink paintings have won awards. She received a writing fellowship from Waypoint Foundation to spend time at one of their Key Largo retreats. This is her first book.

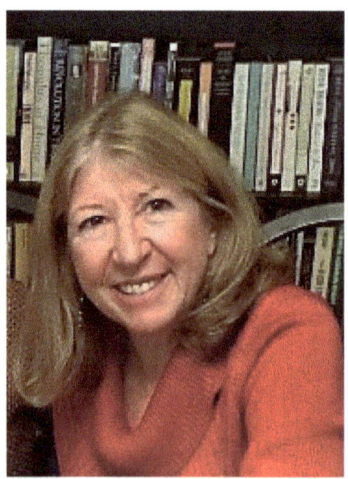

Hilary Bartlett, author. Ann Sutter.

www.ingramcontent.com/pod-product-compliance
Lightning Source LLC
Chambersburg PA
CBHW040516220526
45473CB00012B/2884